COMMUNICATE

EXPERIENCE HIM.   SHARE HIM.

TERRY K. BROWN
AND MICHAEL ROSS

PROMISE PRESS
An Imprint of Barbour Publishing

Published by Promise Press, an imprint of Barbour Publishing, Inc., P.O. Box 719, Uhrichsville, Ohio 44683, www.promisepress.com

ecpa Member of the
Evangelical Christian
Publishers Association

Printed in the United States of America.

5 4 3 2 1

COMMUNICATE

Dedicated to the men in my life.
To my husband, Mark,
My three sons, Nathan, Ryan, and Brennan,
And especially to my Savior, Jesus Christ,
The Man who gave His life to the world
To give us eternal life.
Thank You for giving me the opportunity
to *Communicate* Your message.

—Terry K. Brown

To Christopher, my son.
It's my prayer that your life shines strong for Jesus.
In fact, your name means "Christ Bearer."

—Michael Ross

contents

acknowledgments

Terry K. Brown would like to thank everyone who has worked so hard on this project:

Tim Martins, Shannon Hill and the entire staff at Barbour Publishing. Thank you for your patience, creative input, and insight. Thank you for giving me the awesome opportunity to *Communicate* Christ.

Michael Ross of Focus on the Family. Thank you for taking charge of this book. I'm honored to have worked with you.

Jama Kehoe Bigger, my friend and co-writer on the devotions for the *Communicate Christ* journal.

Pastor Gregg Parris and my Life Group at Union Chapel. Laura, Dave, Beth, Rick, Sarah and Mark. Thank you for the prayers and encouragement.

Thomas Gibson, Kevin Short, Bob Beasley, and Mike Hauk.

Jim Borgmann and the entire Defur, Voran Firm.

Dicksons Gifts.

JJI International.

Spinweb Designs and Brian Wilson in the development of the Web site.

Robyn Martins of Barbour Publishing for the cover designs and creative input.

Steve Reno and Sarah Mezo.

My family. Thank you.

My husband, Mark Patterson, and Patterson/Thomas, Inc. Thank you for all the long hours, work, support, prayers, and encouragement throughout the entire process.

foreword

the great commission and you!
(some thoughts from AUDIO ADRENALINE)

"Therefore go and make disciples of all nations, baptizing them in the name of the Father and of the Son and of the Holy Spirit, and teaching them to obey everything I have commanded you. And surely I am with you always, to the very end of the age."
MATTHEW 28:19–20

The Great Commission—that's where Christians come in. Actually, that's where we go out. Jesus wants us to get our feet moving, to tell the world that humanity doesn't have to live a lonely, miserable existence. Our Savior offers everyone hope, happiness, healing, and—best of all—heaven. Eternal life with Him!

But if you're anything like us, you've probably discovered that sharing history's greatest news is hard. You open your mouth to talk about Christ. . .but the words somehow get stuck. And your mind races with all kinds of crazy thoughts: *Exactly what should I say? What if they ask questions that I can't answer? Maybe I'm too young to talk to my friends about something this important.*

Guess what? You're not alone. Throughout the ages, God has called people who felt completely inadequate to be His mouthpiece. The truth is, He doesn't need our ability; He needs our willingness. And that's what this book is all about—equipping and encouraging you to be available— allowing Christ to communicate the Good News through you. We've echoed this message through the years in our song, "Hands and Feet." Now you have a book that offers a solid plan.

So read on! Sharing your faith is the greatest journey of all! It's our prayer that these pages will equip you to be a radical witness.

MARK STUART, WILL MCGINNISS,
TYLER BURKUM, BEN CISSELL
AUDIO ADRENALINE

starting point
how to communicate

Even though we live in an information age—an era in which thoughts, ideas, and communication move around the globe instantaneously—isn't it strange that we still get tongue-tied when it comes to transmitting the gospel? And despite all the high-tech toys at our fingertips. . .despite having access to E-mail, cellular phones, voice mail, and the Internet. . .billions of people still haven't heard the hope of Jesus Christ.

The question is, *What are we communicating?*

As Christians, we've been entrusted with the awesome privilege sharing our faith with the world. We are called to be reflections of Christ, not only through our words, but through our actions, as well. What we do and what we say really does matter.

But how do we communicate the gospel effectively? You're holding the answer—*Communicate.*

This book is part of the Communicate Christ program—a line of products that include the Communicate Christ medallion, and the Communicate Christ Web site.

The Medallion: Wear It. Give It. Track It.

Each medallion is individually numbered on the reverse side, and includes the Internet Web site address, www.communicatechrist.com. No two have the same number! As with any *Communicate* jewelry (available in stores everywhere), you can visit the Web site and register specific information about your medallion. The information includes: medallion number, name, address, age, and comments.

The next step is witnessing. If someone you witness to accepts Christ as his Lord and Savior, you can pass the medallion on to him. The new owner then logs on to the www.communicatechrist.com site and registers his information. And the process continues. After time has passed, the original owner can track his medallion to follow how many people have committed their lives to Jesus Christ.

The Website: www.communicatechrist.com

Log on and watch others come to Christ (as their medallions are passed along to others over time). This site offers exciting information for all believers, old and new. You'll find testimonies, comments, apologetics, online sermons, Christian chat rooms, and message boards.

This Book: Communicate

In addition to being a twenty-eight-day devotional and journal, this resource presents a practical, relevant way of sharing the truth of Jesus Christ. It follows our Savior's example throughout the Bible of using personal stories, especially a believer's lifestyle, as a way of connecting with others—and, ultimately, connecting them to the One who gives eternal life.

Bottom line: Even if we feel inadequate evangelizing, and despite the reality of not having all the answers, we each have a story to tell; one that testifies to the eternal glory, the transforming power and the timeless truth of humanity's only Savior—Jesus Christ.

May the Lord bless your walk as you begin to communicate Christ with your life. Remember, by leading one person to Christ, you can lead nations to the absolute truth of God!

May the God who gives endurance and encouragement give you a spirit of unity among yourselves as you follow Christ Jesus, so that with one heart and mouth you may glorify the God and Father of our Lord Jesus Christ.

ROMANS 15:5

witness *with* words

Kellie scrunches into a tiny ball and rests her chin on her knee. The conversation between her history study partners is almost too much to handle.

"Are you sure, Sarah?" Danielle presses. "I mean, you could be a little late because of midterms, stress—stuff like that."

"Look, I'm not just a little late. Trust me, I know what's happening inside my own body." Sarah puts her hand on her stomach and looks down. "I'm about fourteen weeks along."

"Have you told your parents?" Melanie asks.

"Are you kidding?! They'd freak."

"How about. . .him?" Danielle adds.

Sarah shakes her head. "No."

A stabbing pain shoots through Kellie's stomach as she listens. She just can't imagine facing such a hard dilemma. Yet, as a Christian, Kellie knows that Christ is the solution to any problem in life. But how can she express this to her hurting friend?

Kellie leans back and squeezes her eyes shut. Lord, I know I'm supposed to be Your hands and feet—but I don't know where to begin. What should I say? How should I reach out?

Why is Jeremy's heart pounding? He's hanging out at a coffeehouse with a couple of new friends from school, and, suddenly, the subject changes to religion.

"Why do Christians think they have the only ticket to heaven?" says one of the guys. "I mean, the Bible is just a bunch of fairy tales."

"I know what you mean," says another guy. "And what's pathetic is, most Christians don't realize that they're narrow-minded hypocrites. Why should I believe what they say?"

Jeremy, who just happens to be serious about his relationship with Christ, keeps his mouth shut. But as he leaves the coffeehouse, he carries with him a lot of unidentified emotions—not to mention a bunch of guilt.

♦   ♦   ♦   ♦

Sweaty palms. A pounding chest. Desperate gasps for air.

What some might mistake as a heart attack could very well be a Christian's attempt to share what's in his heart. Just ask Kellie and Jeremy.

When it comes to communicating the greatest news of all—eternal freedom through Jesus Christ—most of us feel clueless, speechless. . .and totally ineffective.

♦ We fear we'll mess up what God accomplished through the cross.

- We obsess over appearances.

- We treat non-Christians like projects instead of people.

- We speak an alien language—known by insiders as "Christianese."

And too often, our lives don't come close to matching what we claim we believe about God and the Bible. Yet, regardless of how weak or inadequate we feel, Christ has given each of His followers an important mission: "We are therefore Christ's ambassadors, as though God were making his appeal through us" (2 Corinthians 5:20).

He didn't call us to hide in a Christian huddle—or to be part of His "secret service." As Christians, we've grounded our lives on what the Bible says, which means we're convinced that humankind is more than just a cosmic accident. Jesus Christ is transforming our lives, and we've got to tell the world about it.

Sharing our faith should be the most natural thing in the world, because it's really nothing more than telling someone else the story of what God has done for us. When we talk about Jesus with another person, we are sharing our faith. When we tell the story of our spiritual journey in front of a group, we are sharing our faith. When we tell people about Jesus in a letter or E-mail, we are sharing our faith.

In fact, the Lord actually wants us to create occasions in which to talk about Him, seizing every opportunity to share our faith, witnessing where we are. In other words, take a meal over to a neighbor whose husband is in the hospital. Stay in touch with a coworker who is going through rough times. Drive an elderly lady to her doctor's appointment. Casual contacts with acquaintances and neighbors are usually more effective than witnessing to strangers. Your caring attitude can create open doors through which Jesus Christ can enter as Savior and Lord.

goin' public with God

You've been serving up grande lattes and double-decaf-mocha cappuccinos at Starbucks for about a month. You work from 6:00 to 10:00, three nights a week, and then you put in eight hours every Saturday. The Starbucks manager has asked you to work Sundays, but you've told him you can't because you go to church and want to spend time with your family.

Your boss hasn't forced you to take on Sundays yet, though you can tell he isn't happy about being turned down.

One Saturday afternoon, at about 2 P.M., you take your thirty-minute lunch in the break room. Because it's a slow time of the day, about five people are hanging out with you. The conversation moves to what everyone is doing on Sunday. Julie, one of the older women, mentions that after church she and her family are going for a drive in the country.

"Church," the manager says. "I wouldn't be caught dead in church. It's too full of hypocrites!"

This starts a flow of complaints about Christianity. One of the younger checkout women says she used to go but they always talked too much about hell. "I thought church was a place where people were supposed to love each other. All I ever felt there was judgment," she says.

A guy your age says he can't believe people actually would want to follow an old, hard-to-read book.

Julie speaks up: "I just think you've all had bad experiences. Church is great. Forty years ago I heard that Jesus Christ loved me enough to die for my sins so I could go to heaven. Church helps me learn more about God. It also provides a place where I can help others. And that's what church is all about."

"Help others—right!" the manager scoffs. "We all know what the church is really after: our hard-earned money—especially those cheesy televangelists." Suddenly, he looks at you. "Hey, you go to church every week. Why? Is it because your parents force you?"

"Uhhh. . ." You stand there speechless, with all eyes on you. Julie smiles, while your boss grimaces. You swallow.

What do I say, God? I'm stuck!

solid reasons to speak up [1]

Knowing what to say and do without looking like a wishy-washy Christian isn't easy.

If we were confident that there wouldn't be any social—or sometimes economic—consequences when we attempt to represent the Christian faith, most would know the right actions to take or words to speak. Ah, but sometimes there *are* consequences, aren't there? So we keep silent or say something that betrays what we know to be true. In the process, we feel guilty or stupid. What's the answer? Here are a few ideas on how to keep firm when your knees are weak:

1. Rehearse.

With a parent, friend, or youth leader, go through as many situations you can think of that could cause you to do the wrong thing when a dilemma hits. If you know what to expect and what to say—*before* it happens—you'll be much more confident.

"But in your hearts set apart Christ as Lord. Always be prepared to give an answer to everyone who asks you to give the reason for the hope that you have. But do this with gentleness and respect, keeping a clear conscience, so that those who speak maliciously against your good behavior in Christ may be ashamed of their slander" (1 Peter 3:15–16).

2. Get the word out.

Unfortunately, many Christians want to be full-time in God's Secret Service and hide their faith. But you don't have to hand out tracts with your testimony on them to inform your coworkers of your allegiance to Christ. Instead, drop a few signals:

▶ Ask questions: "Does your family have any Christmas (Easter) traditions? We go to church on Christmas Eve and. . ." (See chapter 3 for more ideas on questions to ask.)

▶ Read a pocket Bible or a Christian book on your break.

▶ When someone mentions a struggle he's going through, let him know you'll pray for him. How? A short note or quick word is often all it takes.

"I am not ashamed of the gospel, because it is the power of God for the salvation of everyone who believes: first for the Jew, then for the Gentile" (Romans 1:16).

3. Let your actions speak loudly.

Your tasks at work come first. If you're not a good employee, you may end up giving all Christians a bad name. You're not a slave, but this verse applies nonetheless:

"Slaves, obey your earthly masters in everything; and do it, not only when their eye is on you and to win their favor, but with sincerity of heart and reverence for the Lord" (Colossians 3:22).

4. Hold your tongue.

When other workers start telling off-color jokes or making crude remarks, fight the urge to participate. Don't act superior or judgmental (after all, non-Christians *will* act like non-Christians); just try to keep quiet or turn away. Yes, it may mean it will take longer to be included in the group, but in the long run, what type of reputation do you want—a sheep who'll blend in with the gang because it's safe, or a person of character who has a firm moral foundation?

"Do not let any unwholesome talk come out of your mouths, but only what is helpful for building others up according to their needs, that it may benefit those who listen. . . . Nor should there be obscenity, foolish talk or coarse joking, which are out of place, but rather thanksgiving" (Ephesians 4:29, 5:4).

how to lead
someone to Christ

Your sin keeps you from having a personal relationship with God. (See Romans 3:23.)

What is sin?

Jesus Christ died and rose again so that your sins could be forgiven. (See 1 Peter 3:18.)

Why do we need the Savior?

You must accept God's gift of grace. You must also trust Jesus to be your Savior and to forgive you of your sins. (See John 1:12.)

What does it mean to be forgiven?

You have the promise of eternal life with Him and a crown of righteousness! (See 1 John 5:13.)

What is eternal life?

You can now begin a new life in Christ! You can grow in His love, peace, strength, and knowledge. Begin your great adventure now by letting Him guide every step you take. (See 2 Peter 3:18.)

what does a new life in Christ mean to you personally?

real-life story

Bible boy strikes again![2]

"Hey, Bible Boy. Where's your Word?" shouts a voice from across the crowded hall.

Fifteen-year-old Eric Stueberg grins and holds up a tattered book with fluorescent lime green words— HOLY BIBLE—handwritten across the cover.

"Right here," he says. "Wouldn't leave home without it!"

It's Monday morning at Florida's Fort Walton Beach High School, and Eric loves his new reputation. While other guys return from the weekend bragging about how far they've gone with a girl or how much they've drank, Eric can't stop boasting about his radical God. . .and how far Christ can take a life that's fired up for Him.

It all started a few months back when Eric and some of his church friends realized they had work to do for God—starting with their own lives.

"During one of our revival services, the Lord came and His Spirit poured out on our church. It was amazing," Eric says. "And when the pastor invited people to the altar, my friends and I knew we needed to go forward."

The message from Revelation 3:15—about being lukewarm—had touched a nerve. Eric realized that he wasn't on track with Jesus, and that attending church on Sundays and Wednesdays wasn't enough.

"You have to *know* Jesus," Eric says. "He has to be your best friend—your Lord.

"I thought about how half the kids in my school weren't saved," Eric continues. "I knew I needed to make a change in my life, then reach out to other teens. I finally stood up and went down to the altar. Everything just broke. It was a real turnabout."

One of the first things Eric and his friend, Julie Bronson, did was start a Bible study at school. The second—and most important, he says—was to step out as a "walking billboard."

"Some teens wear Christian T-shirts and go to church, but they also spend their weekends partying," Eric says. "I used to be that way too. But I've seen how it can completely ruin a Christian's witness."

Today, he's convinced that if you're gonna claim to be a Christian, you'd better live like one. After all, being a walking billboard means having your life read by others. "I want people to read 'JESUS' when they see me," he says. "That's why I love being called 'Bible Boy.' It's cool."

But being radical for God comes at a cost. Eric lost a few friends who thought he'd become too religious, and he occasionally gets picked on. "Let's not kid ourselves; taking a stand for God is far from easy," Eric says. "But who says following Jesus should be easy?"

The first few weeks were the hardest. But, gradually, casual friends began calling him Bible Boy—with a positive tone—and some even visited his campus Bible study. And what began as a handful of teens who would spend their lunch hour praying, now fills up a room.

"This world needs bold Christians," Eric says, "especially teenagers who are willing to stand in the face of what's popular and say, 'Jesus is the *only* truth, the *only* life, and the *only* way.'

"As far as being rejected, I don't want to stand before God on Judgment Day and hear the words, 'I counted on you to tell your friends about Me, but you didn't.'

"I don't want my friends to spend eternity in hell. I can't be selfish. I've got to speak up. . .and do my part to rock my school for Christ."

And Eric's commitment is making an impact. "Today, I'm not the only 'Bible Boy' at school," he says. "There's a lot of us now. And that's awesome."

how to start a Christian club

Fifteen-year-old Eric Stueberg took a bold step by starting a campus Bible study group—and you can too!

But remember: The purpose of starting a Christian club is not to create a "holy huddle" or a special clique, but to be a light where God has placed you—and to love and to serve your campus for Christ.

As Eric discovered, not every student will want to join. But as you begin to meet needs on your campus, some will want to know more about the One who loves them most—and who can meet the deepest needs of their hearts.

So, how should you get started?

1. **Pray with friends.**

2. **Pick a name.**

3. **Select a sponsor.**

4. **Choose an encourager.**

5. **Prepare a constitution.**

6. **Present a proposal to your school's authorities.**

7. **Publicize your new club.**

Information gathered from See You at the Pole Ministries, Forth Worth, Texas.

chapter two

witness *without* words

"How has being a Christian changed your life?"

The question catches Alicia off guard, causing her to gag on her salad. She takes a big gulp of water, clears her throat, and attempts to give an answer. "Well, uh, lots of ways—"

It's lunchtime, and Alicia and her friend Holly—a coworker at the mall department store where Alicia works—are grabbing a quick bite at their favorite food court hangout. On most days, they spend their thirty-minute breaks people-watching and laughing about last weekend's "I-hate-being-dateless" ice cream/sympathy binge.

But today, the conversation goes deeper.

"Look, Alicia," Holly interrupts. "We've worked together for six months. I'd say we're getting to be pretty good friends."

Alicia smiles. "Of course!"

"And since you know me so well, you know that I'm not religious—and that I don't plan to be."

Alicia smiles again. "I understand."

"But you're so into God and church and stuff," Holly says. "Even though you've never tried to push that on me, I watch you—your life, I mean. And I see something different in you—something I admire. So I've got to know: Exactly how has being a Christian changed your life?"

Alicia leans forward and takes a deep breath. "First of all," she says, "I need you to know something: I'm not religious either. I have a relationship—a relationship with Jesus Christ. He's changed my life in lots of ways, both big and small. He's given me hope, purpose—eternity. He's forgiven me for all the stupid things I've ever done or thought. He's shown me what love—authentic love—is all about."

Slowly, Alicia's anxieties about being a perfect witness and saying all the right things melt away. Instead, she communicates naturally—friend to friend, soul to soul. Alicia talks, and Holly listens—it's as simple as that.

♦   ♦   ♦   ♦

As Alicia shared her faith, she didn't use big words or debate lofty doctrines. She merely told her story and gave Holly a glimpse into her heart. Yet it was Alicia's lifestyle that paved the way. She lived her faith consistently through her words *and her actions.*

And as Holly commented, "I watch you—your life, I mean. And I see something different in you—something I admire."

This is the core of evangelism. As Christians, we are called to be out in the open, living as witnesses for Christ in every part of our lives—at school, at work, even when we recreate. Wherever we go, God wants to use us to spread "everywhere the fragrance of the knowledge of him" (2 Corinthians 2:14). Our highest calling is to be salt, light, and a good-smelling fragrance that attracts people to God.

don't stay in a holy huddle

Or to put it more bluntly, "Flee your Christian ghetto."

In his book *Roaring Lambs,* Dallas-based TV producer Bob Briner compares the Christian Church (and its media subculture) to a ghetto that the rest of society either avoids altogether or races through on their way to another part of town. Before his death in the late nineties, Briner was a shining example of a believer who lived his faith well beyond the fringes of the church. He was convinced that communicating the gospel is a 24/7 pursuit that happens most effectively through "countless ordinary people in countless ordinary ways out in the real world"—not through lofty theology that's preached from a pulpit. Yet Briner was frustrated. He wasn't sure if Christians really understood this.

"It's almost as if we believe God is strong enough to take care of His own only as long as they stay within the safety of the Christian ghetto," he wrote. "And yet, the Bible gives us countless examples of people like Joseph, who not only served as an advisor to the 'president' of his day but also used that position to influence the entire land. Can't we do that today?"[3]

Several years earlier, and nearly four thousand miles across the Atlantic Ocean, a bishop in the Church of England, Stephen Neill, also warned that too many Christians hide in their sanctuaries: "How do we make contact with the real outsider, and to what kind of message is it likely that he will give an ear? . . . Most of our so-called evangelism takes place within or on the fringes of the church; we do not seem yet to have found the way to break out of the Christian ghetto and into the world."[4]

Living our lives in a holy huddle makes us feel safe— even comfortable. When our focus is on the huddle, we don't have to deal with scary people on the outside. But get this: Our comfort has a very low biblical priority. Throughout the Gospels we see examples of Christ making His disciples uncomfortable by befriending scary people—outcasts. True, Jesus doesn't want us to get pulled down by the wrong crowd. Instead, He wants us to extend a helping hand and to pull others up.

Think about modern-day outcasts: the handicapped person who is often overlooked or the loner who feels subhuman. Would Jesus visit these people? Would He know their names, care about them, tell them stories? He would—and you should too. Here's how 2 Corinthians 2:15 describes our Christian witness: "For we are to God the aroma of Christ among those who are being saved and those who are perishing." And in Jesus' own words, we are called to be salt and light: "You are the salt of the earth. . . . You are the light of the world. A city on a hill cannot be hidden. Neither do people light a lamp and put it under a bowl. Instead they put it on its stand, and it gives light to everyone in the house. In the same way, let your light shine before men, that they may see your good deeds and praise your Father in heaven" (Matthew 5:13–16).

get off your "can't" and get going!

So, exactly how should we break out of our holy huddles and be salt and light in the world? Again, the answer comes straight from the words and actions of Jesus.

While our Savior's first call is to " 'Come, follow me' " (Matthew 4:19), His second is to "Go"—" 'Go into all the world and preach the Good News to all creation' " (Mark 16:15). And before He sent His disciples, He instructed them on how they should witness: " 'I am sending you out like sheep among wolves. Therefore be as shrewd as snakes and as innocent as doves' " (Matthew 10:16). In other words, if we want to move beyond the walls of the church and truly go into the world, we must be grounded in God *and* perceptive to current culture.

Be compassionate.

Observe those within your sphere of influence—family, friends, students, and coworkers. Learn what motivates them, what they value and believe—especially how they live. Then look for creative, relevant ways of being Christ's "hands and feet" in their world. And as you witness, never treat nonbelievers as a project. "Jesus replied: ' "Love the Lord your God with all your heart and with all your soul and with all your mind." This is the first and greatest commandment. And the second is like it: " 'Love your neighbor as yourself" ' " (Matthew 22:37–39).

Be consistent.

Is your walk in sync with your talk? Are you "as innocent as doves"? Is your life a reflection of Jesus? Witnessing is all about telling *and showing* others what Jesus is like. You can tell them by what you say, but you show them by your own conduct.

"Be very careful, then, how you live—not as unwise but as wise, making the most of every opportunity, because the days are evil. Therefore, do not be foolish, but understand what the Lord's will is. Do not get drunk on wine, which leads to debauchery. Instead, be filled with the Spirit. Speak to one another with psalms, hymns and spiritual songs. Sing and make music in your heart to the Lord, always giving thanks to God the Father for everything, in the name of our Lord Jesus Christ" (Ephesians 5:15–20).

Be bold.

Never let fear hold you back from befriending an unbeliever. Consider the observations of legendary evangelist Billy Graham: "It is fear that makes us unwilling to listen to another's point of view, fear that our own ideas may be attacked. Jesus had no such fear, no such pettiness of viewpoint, no need to fence Himself off for His own protection. He knew the difference between graciousness and compromise and we would do well to learn from Him."[5]

skate your witness

Or *sing* it or *cook* it or *drive* it! Maybe art is your thing—or computers or extreme sports or science. Regardless, take inventory of your skills and interests, even the stuff you do for fun—then use them as tools for God.

That's exactly how Christian science-writer Fred Heeren operates with the skeptics he encounters. "The greatest scientific discoveries of our century make great conversation starters for the Christian witness," he explains in his book *Show Me God.* "It makes good sense to begin with facts that both believers and unbelievers can agree upon. And then, the separate realms of science and faith can actually be used to [a Christian's] advantage. To begin to share one's faith, one needs only to show how modern science has raised questions it can't answer. . . . This is where science ends. And this is where the Bible begins."

Bottom line: Discover ways of allowing the Holy Spirit to touch others through your lifestyle—instead of just blending into the crowd. "Do your best to present yourself to God as one approved, a workman who does not need to be ashamed and who correctly handles the word of truth" (2 Timothy 2:15).

Here's how some guys and girls are using their talents as a launching pad for the truth at school, at work, and on the playing field:

▶ **COMMUNICATE CHRIST through music:** Brian, twenty-one, of Paris, France, sings in coffeehouses and at festivals. "My family are missionaries in France. People in this country don't easily trust strangers—especially the church. But I've discovered that my music breaks down barriers—and even allows me to preach a sermon."

▶ **COMMUNICATE CHRIST through service:** Kirsten, seventeen, of Los Angeles, volunteers at animal shelters throughout Southern California. "I work with a group that cares for stray animals. I do my best to demonstrate Christ's love through my actions, as well as my compassion for His creation. And every day, He opens doors for me to witness."

▶ **COMMUNICATE CHRIST through sports:** Susan, eighteen, of Denver, is a professional rock climber. "My attitude means everything during competition. All eyes are on me—so I do my best to behave as Jesus would."

- **COMMUNICATE CHRIST through entertainment:** Jordan, twenty-two, of Orlando, is a skilled puppeteer. "The arts are so neglected by Christians. It's truly a mission field. I witness daily through my walk—the way I treat others and my integrity."

- **COMMUNICATE CHRIST through adventure:** Will, sixteen, of Dallas, is an avid outdoorsman. "Hand me a backpack and put me on a trail somewhere deep in the wilderness, and I'm a happy man! It's amazing how the wilderness can open the doors for conversations about Christ. Each summer, I go on outdoor treks. I do my best to point others to the fingerprints of God."

▶　　▶　　▶　　▶

Sharing your faith through your lifestyle really isn't a big mystery. In fact, it should come naturally for Christians. Just ask Vince Flumiani, a twenty-something founder of Jedidiah Boardriding Company in San Diego, California.

Though most of the board riders he meets would rather be slimed by seaweed than go to church, he's found that Jedidiah has given him an in. "When I go to skate parks and appear in lineups with other surfers, they talk to me about church and say, 'Christians are hypocrites; I won't go there.'"

So Vince goes to them. He hangs with them, is willing to "get messy" and hurt with them, and learns their stories. He even creates products that will appeal to their tastes, hoping they'll question Jedidiah's message and wonder about the peace he's found.

"That's my passion," Vince says. "We're not a Christian clothing company—we're a boardriding company that's about Jesus Christ. We know God's never failed us. He's given us something better, and that's what I want to tell everyone."

In the words of Bob Briner, "It's not only possible but absolutely necessary for Christians and Christian values to become a vital element in the overall moral and cultural discourse of our nation. Without our strategic involvement in the culture-shaping areas of art, entertainment, the media, education, and the like, this nation simply cannot be the great and glorious society it once was. If we are to be obedient to our Lord's call to go into all the world, we will begin reentering the fields that we have left."

◆　　　◆　　　◆　　　◆

We're impressed with Vince's passion to combine surfing and skating with ministry. He's even given us an idea: Wouldn't it be great if you followed his example and used your interests to witness for God? You may not yet be a pro, but you're definitely a champion if—like Vince—you've taken the gutsy, tough steps that help make a difference in someone's life.

Whether you surf or sing, here are some ideas on how you can use just about any activity to witness for God.

▸ **Forget "Christianese"**—try communicating in their language. "I use surfing metaphors to illustrate how sin separates us from God," Vince says. "I've discovered that surfers are more ministered to by what they see rather than what they hear."

- **Be a good sport.** Face it, your actions often speak louder than words. How do you act when you're at the skate park or on the basketball court? Make an effort to never turn any competition into a contest that proves who's superior. Switch your goal from "clobbering the competition" to making a good move or shot, playing by the rules, or improving your skills.

- **Involve your huddle.** There's strength in numbers. Besides, getting your Christian friends involved can open the door to greater ministry. You can be like an army that can rise up among the extreme sports culture. (Or among guys and girls on the basketball court, or in the science lab, or—well, ah, you get the picture.)

- **When people look at your life, make sure they see. . .**

   . . .someone constantly dying to Jesus.

   . . .a person of integrity who dares to put his or her life on the line for the gospel.

   . . .a person with a sincere heart—not a guy hiding behind a mask.

- **Be real with God—and others.** Too many Christians mistakenly believe that God doesn't want them to be honest about their lives. They think that He will be upset if they tell Him how they really feel. But the Scriptures tell us that God does not want you to be superficial—in your relationship with Him, with others, or in your own life. In Psalm 51:6, David writes, "Surely you desire truth in the inner parts; you teach me wisdom in the inmost place."

Be honest about your pain, confusion, or doubt—even with people you're trying to reach with the gospel. You aren't expected to have all the answers—just a committed, searching heart.

The fact is, God desires truth and honesty at the deepest level and wants you to experience His love, forgiveness, and power in *all* areas of your life. Experiencing and sharing His love doesn't mean that all of your thoughts, emotions, and behaviors will hit the mark every time. It means that you can be *real,* feeling pain and joy, love and anger, confidence and confusion. It's this kind of honesty that will attract others to the gospel.

pray for your friends

In Romans 9:1–3, Paul wrote that he cared so much about his unbelieving friends that he would be willing to exchange places with them and actually go to hell so that they could be with Jesus in heaven. Imagine having that kind of compassion for others! As for your friends, love them enough to pray for them. Ask Christ to open their eyes and hearts to receiving the truth.

Prayer is a critical element to help spread the gospel message. Think of it this way: As a gardener tills the soil so he can plant seeds, likewise, prayer tills the soil of our hearts to prepare us for God's message of salvation.

All around you are family members, friends, and acquaintances who do not know Christ as their Lord and Savior. You need to pray for them, then step out and share the Good News of salvation!

You see, Jesus' whole purpose for coming to earth was to redeem us, His children, from the sin that had doomed us from the beginning of time. There was a huge, Grand Canyon-like gulf between us and God, and nothing could bring us back together. That is, nothing except the shed blood of Jesus Christ, God's only Son.

rev up for revival

Nobody can start a revival except God. But you can prepare for one. Like Hezekiah who sought the Lord, you can come to God just as you are, with everything that concerns you, saddens you, and moves you about the condition of our nation today. You can prepare yourself for your own personal revival by asking yourself some very basic questions:

- Was there ever a time when I placed my trust in Jesus Christ alone to save me?

- Are my personal devotions consistent and meaningful?

- Do I practically apply God's Word to my everyday life?

- Am I quick to recognize and agree with God in confession when I have sinned?

- Am I quick to admit to others when I am wrong?

- Do I consistently obey what I know God wants me to do?

- Do I consistently obey the human authorities God has placed over my life (those who do not contradict God's moral law)?

- Am I willing to give up all sin for God?

- Does my schedule reveal that God is first in my life?

- Is there consistent evidence of the fruit of the Spirit being produced in my life?

- Am I more concerned about pleasing God than other people?

- Do I keep my mind free from any entertainment that could stimulate impure thoughts?

- Do I have a burden for those who don't know Christ?

"Rev Up for Revival" was inspired by the book *Revival Signs* © 1995 by Tom Phillips and Vision House Publishing Inc.

real-life
story

taking a SWAT at satan

Mark Mynheir is a former SWAT team officer in Palm Bay, Florida. His world revolved around busting bad guys—from surrounding a barricaded gunman to locking down on a full-fledged hostage situation. God was a stranger to him. That is, until he met two committed Christians—who were also SWAT team members. Here's Mark's story in his own words.

Most of the guys on my SWAT team were prior military: Marines and Special Forces types. The other team members were experienced police officers who had paid their dues and had proven themselves on the streets. We all shared a common bond—we would go places and do things that most people in their right minds would never imagine.

From serving search warrants on crack houses to surrounding a barricaded gunman, or locking down on a full-fledged hostage situation, our SWAT team was called to deal with the dirtiest of dirty jobs. In spite of those things—or *because* of those things—I truly enjoyed my job. Yet in this environment of macho cops and hardened criminals, something quite unexpected happened: God started turning my heart toward Him.

true grit: serving God

At the time, I was a young, arrogant cop. As a former Marine and wannabe tough guy, my world revolved around busting bad guys. Spiritual issues were far from me.

That all started to change when I was on the team. Two other members—Jim and Ernie—were committed Christians. I was not, and to my shame, it showed. Every day during our training, I would lead the team in raunchy conversations. Our training days always seemed to degenerate into one big cuss-fest, as each man would try to outdo the other. But in this environment, I was king. I could be filthier, nastier, and tell raunchier stories than anyone. But as I sat on my podium, spewing out whatever depraved joke came to mind, Jim and Ernie trained quietly, never joining the pathetic display. As I would tell my stories or just talk trash, I would glance toward Jim and Ernie, and I would see them fervently doing their duty. Their silence convicted me. They never rebuked or confronted me; they didn't have to. Their example was making a difference in my heart, but I didn't think I had the power to stop. I was twenty-seven, and I was still worried about impressing my friends. That wasn't an issue for Jim and Ernie.

from tough guy to tough faith

Before we would step off on an operation, Jim and Ernie would pray together. The rest of us would laugh or say things under our breath, many times mocking them outright. In spite of that, Jim and Ernie were always faithful—as team members and as friends. They were the first ones there if someone had a problem or needed help, and they more than pulled their weight on the team. Every day they walked in integrity. They were genuine. Soon, even the little razzing we gave them about their faith stopped. It's hard to find fault with someone when they're the real thing.

During this time, Ernie and Jim began witnessing to me, telling me little things here and there about Jesus and faith. It didn't come off as preachy or self-righteous. They were my friends who would gladly take a bullet for me. I trusted them. And I listened.

And when my world began to crumble, I remembered all the things those around me—especially Jim and Ernie—had told me about salvation and getting right with God. I got on my knees and gave my life to Christ. After that, I sought Jim and Ernie out, so they could be the first people I told.

Things changed almost immediately—on the team and in my life. First, I lost half my vocabulary. But it didn't take long to get used to the English language without all of the expletives and colorful adjectives.

Second, the dynamics of the team changed as well. I started praying with Jim and Ernie before our operations. It was a little strange at first, but I grew into it. Before I left that team, more people were praying with us than not. We joked that we would put "Jesus saves" on our battering ram, to leave a more positive imprint on the lives of the people we visited.

From that original fifteen-man team, six more team members, myself included, became committed Christians, and the gospel was clearly presented to the others. All because two men chose to walk in integrity and bring the torch of Christ into some very dark places.

key questions to ask

"Don't look down!" Christopher tells himself over and over. "Stay focused on the goal—just as Zach showed me. I won't get stuck. I won't fall. I can do this."

Christopher reaches above his head and grips a tiny crevice with his fingertips and slowly makes his way up the steep rock face—inch by inch.

"This is insane!" the eighteen year old mumbles to himself. "How'd I ever get talked into being a 'human insect'?!"

"Go, 'Spiderman'!" his buddy hollers down from a ledge forty feet above, grinning from ear to ear. "You're climbing like a pro."

A pro? Hardly! But the encouragement from Zach feels good. It gives Christopher confidence and keeps him going as he attempts his first "spring break climbing expedition."

For some reason, the two guys really hit it off— which, to Christopher, is nothing short of strange. Both are college freshmen and share a dorm room, but that's all they have in common. Christopher is an English major who's into art and literature. Zach is "Mr. Extreme": an experienced rock climber who hopes to one day turn his phys ed education into a wilderness travel career.

The two are worlds apart spiritually, as well. Christopher is committed to his faith in Jesus. (Even his name means "Christ bearer.") Zach isn't sure what he believes.

Christopher's mind flashes back to the conversation that convinced him to spend a day hanging from a remote cliff in the middle of the Utah desert:

"Tell you what," Zach said to Christopher just before spring break. "Go climbing with me in Moab, Utah, and I'll go to church with you. I'll even listen to your endless sermons about this Jesus dude, instead of blanking out—which is what I usually do."

Christopher smiled and stuck out his hand. "Deal."

Now the big day is here, and the "artist-turned-climber" feels as if he's in way over his head—literally!

Suddenly, panic. "Uh. . .I need help, Zach!" Christopher yells. "There's no place to go! I'm stuck!"

He has reached a point on the wall that's smooth and slippery. Adrenaline surges through his veins, and every muscle seems to tremble.

"Think it through," Zach says calmly. "Remember what I taught you? Stay focused, take your time, and look for handholds. And trust the rope. If you slip, it will save you."

Christopher spots a tiny groove in the rock face and grips with his fingertips and pushes with his legs.

Then he notices another. . .and another one after that. Before he realizes it, triumph—he joins Zach at the top!

The two high-five each other, then Christopher soaks in the view. He feels pretty confident standing atop the canyon wall.

"The world's amazing from up here, isn't it?" Zach says. "This is where I find my peace."

Christopher glances at Zach and blinks, his buddy's words echoing through his brain. "Okay, man, I met my end of the bargain—now it's your turn."

"Let me guess: It's sermon time," Zach says, handing his friend a Power Bar.

"No, I don't have to preach, 'cause you just did!"

Zach shakes his head. "Now you're talking nonsense, which is probably a sign of oxygen deprivation or overexposure to the sun or—"

"Don't you see, Zach?" Christopher interrupts. "This whole experience has been a sermon. Rock climbing is all about risk and adventure—which is so much like faith in Christ. . .and life itself."

Zach folds his arms and wrinkles his forehead. Christopher keeps talking.

"Just the thought of climbing this canyon wall made me scared out of my mind. But you showed me what to do, and I listened. It was your voice that got me through the rough moments—and the reminder to 'trust the rope.' It took a lot of faith to do this."

Christopher paused, then pointed to some guys across the canyon who were climbing kamikaze style (which means going solo without safety harnesses.) "Check out those climbers. What do you think of them?"

"They're absolute idiots," Zach snapped.

"What makes you say that?"

"Because kamikaze climbing in this canyon is crazy climbing."

"Why's it so crazy? I've seen lots of people going solo today."

"Oh, please. One wrong move and you could slip and—" Zach stops in midsentence and locks gazes with his friend. "Okay, wise guy, I see what you're doing. You're getting me to peach a sermon."

"No sermons," Christopher says with a smile, "just the truth. And that's what Christianity is all about— the truth. Jesus really is my safety line in life, my Guide. . .my Friend."

Zach shakes his head again. "Okay—you're actually making sense to me, which means I'll go to church with you. For once, I'm not blanking out."

Christopher nods his head. "Good. Now, uh, please tell me—how do we get down from here?"

Zach grins extra big. "Time to trust the rope again!"

Christopher would be the first to admit that witnessing is risky business—even scary at times. Yet effective evangelism is all about effective communication. In the New Testament, when Jesus approached the woman at the well who had come to draw water, He spoke to her of living water that would quench her eternal thirst. And in our story above, Christopher used something of interest to his friend to share the gospel—in this case, rock climbing. The point is, our words should be relevant to the person concerned.

And sometimes all it takes to influence a friend for Christ is asking a few key questions at just the right moment. What kinds of questions? Consider these:

twenty questions to get them thinking

- What things in life are most important to you? Why?

- Name a person you look up to the most. What is it about this person that you admire?

- Can I tell you about the person I admire the most—and why?

- What scares you the most about death?

- Do you think there's life after death?

- Name the closest person to you who has died. Where do you think he or she is now?

- Do you believe that there's a heaven and a hell?

- If you died in the next ten seconds, where would you go?

- Do you believe that God created the universe? Why or why not?

- What do you think it means to be a Christian?

- What's the difference between following a religion and having a relationship with Christ?

- Who do you think Jesus is?

- Who is God?

- Have you ever been to church? Describe that experience.

- What do you think you have to do to get to heaven?

- Are people basically good or evil?

- How do you think bad people get to heaven?

- Why do so many people wear crosses? What does the cross mean to you?

- Do you believe Jesus died on a cross? Do you believe He rose from the dead?

excuses you'll encounter

Unfortunately, the same reason people didn't follow Christ when He walked on the earth is the same reason a lot of folks refuse Him today. It has nothing to do with clear thinking or logic or seeing Jesus face-to-face. It doesn't even have to do with proof.

The real reason centers on a person's stubborn will. To acknowledge Jesus as Lord would mean:

1. Having an authority higher than themselves.

It would mean they could no longer run their own lives and live under their own set of rules. They would have to submit their wills to somebody else's; they would have to let God call the shots.

2. Being humbled.

They would have to admit that all of their education and intellect are of no help. The only way they can get into heaven is the old-fashioned way. They have to rely on Christ.

3. Change of lifestyle.

They would have to clean up their acts and obey God.

What are some of the excuses you hear from nonbelievers? Here are a few:

▶ What about all the suffering in the world?

▶ How can I believe in a righteous God when bad things happen to good people?

▶ The church is so boring and irrelevant.

- Christians are hypocrites.

- Christians are arrogant to think they are following absolute truth. What about the truth in other religions?

- Religion just doesn't work.

- I like myself the way I am. I don't want to change.

- I'd lose friends if I suddenly became religious.

You're not expected to have an answer for every excuse you'll hear. "If we could know all about God and His ways of working, He would be no bigger than our finite minds, and not worth believing in," writes David Watson in his book *Called and Committed* (p. 153). "But it is helpful to have some thoughtful and biblical responses to these questions [and comments] to prevent them from becoming excuses, or barriers, to belief."

what to say to a skeptic[6]

The angel said to the women, "Do not be afraid, for I know that you are looking for Jesus, who was crucified. He is not here; he has risen, just as he said. Come and see the place where he lay. Then go quickly and tell his disciples: 'He has risen from the dead and is going ahead of you into Galilee. There you will see him.' Now I have told you."

—MATTHEW 28:5–7

Jesus Christ isn't in the tomb. And get this: The guards are lying on the ground like dead men, and the stone has been rolled away.

Some of the guards get up and race to the chief priests with an amazing story. "There was a violent earthquake at the tomb, and this angel—WHOA! He was bright like lightning and actually rolled away the heavy stone!"

What do the priests do? They bribe the soldiers to lie!

"Tell everyone that you fell asleep and that those pesky disciples stole the body. Above all, don't even mention the stuff about the earthquake and the angel!"

(Check out Matthew 28:1–15 for the full story.)

◆　　　◆　　　◆　　　◆

For centuries people have acted like those stubborn priests and have tried to disprove—even ignore—the resurrection of Jesus Christ. After all, if our Lord didn't rise from the dead, then everything He said and did would be a lie, right? What's more, anybody can claim to be God—psychiatric hospitals are filled with such misguided people. But to say you're God and then *prove* you're immortal—that's another matter.

Christ's resurrection was the proof, the seal of authenticity. And not only have people failed at disproving it, but during their research some have actually become Christians!

Yet the heart of man is often blind. Just look around and you'll spot lots of skeptics. That's why it's important that

Christians be prepared to talk about the greatest event in history. So read on, and let us show you how to lay some groundwork for guiding others to the truth.

Let's take a look at the top three arguments people use—along with some solid answers.

"Maybe Jesus wasn't really dead, and He just rolled away the stone Himself."

Right. A man who has been beaten, tortured, and mutilated for hours is going to lie unattended for two cold nights in a tomb and suddenly find the strength to roll away a two-ton rock, fight off all the Roman soldiers guarding it, then show up convincing everyone that He has a glorious resurrected body. That would be pretty hard to believe.

And while we're talking about His body, let's not forget the blood and water that flowed from His side when the soldier speared it on the cross. If He were alive, the wound would have spurted red blood. But in a dead body, the blood separates into massive red clots and watery serum, just as John described it (see John 19:34).

"Maybe the disciples moved Christ's body."

Hmmm, let's consider the facts: A group of men who have dedicated their lives to a teacher who insisted on truth and honesty are suddenly going to turn into liars and swindlers. And each of these self-seeking no-goods will be willing to face poverty, incredible hardship, torture, and even death to perpetuate that lie. Not a chance.

Then there are the Roman soldiers. Considering that they were the best fighting machines in the world, it's not likely that the disciples could overpower them and knock them all out. But even if they could, why didn't they hurry and race off with the body before the soldiers came to, instead of painstakingly unwrapping all of the burial clothes and neatly folding the facecloth before making their getaway?

"Okay, so maybe the soldiers stole the body."

Hardly. Think about it: The very people who have been assigned to make sure that Jesus' body isn't moved decide to move it. What a neat practical joke to pull on their superiors. Of course, it would mean their execution for becoming traitors, but what's a little death for a laugh or two?

♦   ♦   ♦   ♦

While we're looking at evidence, let's not forget that His resurrection was something Jesus had predicted time and time again. Then, of course, there were all those Old Testament prophecies.

Once we've looked at all the facts and carefully examined the arguments, we would need more faith to believe that Jesus did not rise from the grave than to believe that He did.

outcasts are people too[7]

BY J. MACK STILES

Jesus has a special place in His heart for the outcast. That's who He was. Jesus lived as an outcast. He was despised and rejected and misunderstood and alone. To dismiss the possibility of reaching those who are social outcasts is to risk not knowing Jesus.

Furthermore, when God loves us He is reconciling the outcast to Himself because we were all, at one time, outcasts—"without hope and without God in the world" (Ephesians 2:12). So we mirror God's love for us when we reach out to outcasts.

Here are some steps to help you cross barriers.

1. Take an interest in an outcast's life.

There are nice people who don't dress and look exactly like the guys and girls in your huddle.

2. Cross social hurdles by asking questions.

Investigate their lives and get to know them.

3. Invite them into your world.

Brian invited Ramon to his youth group. It shocked Ramon that a Christian was interested in his life. It seems we spend so much time at religious functions, retreats, and youth group meetings, we barely have time for involvement in others' lives.

4. Find out about their pain.

Fear, pain, and sorrow are all opportunities to talk about how Christ meets our needs.

5. Make a transition to spiritual issues.

Remember, it's okay to just talk and enjoy a conversation with someone. But if the opportunity comes, be ready to pick up on a spiritual topic or even ask spiritual questions if appropriate. If it doesn't happen, that's okay; the Holy Spirit is doing His work at His own speed.

▸   ▸   ▸   ▸

Using questions to cross social hurdles does good things for us. It expands our world. Who wouldn't like to get out of his holy huddle and do some really interesting stuff? It makes us braver. Once you've shared with people inside your sphere, those outside won't seem quite so intimidating.

chapter four

quick quotes
wisdom past and present

 Henry T. Blackaby:
Accept a God-Sized Assignment

"I have come to the place in my life that, if the assignment I sense God is giving me is something that I know I can handle, I know it probably is not from God. The kind of assignments God gives in the Bible are always God-sized. They are always beyond what people can do, because He wants to demonstrate His nature, His strength, His provision, and His kindness to His people and to a watching world. That is the only way the world will come to know Him."

Experiencing God, © 1990, Lifeway Press, p. 116.

 Joy Davidman:
Lead the Dying to Eternal Life

"Our generation has never seen a man crucified except in sugary religious art. . . . A crucified slave beside the Roman road screamed until his voice died and then hung, a filthy, festering clot of flies, sometimes for days—a living man whose hands and feet were swollen masses of gangrenous meat. That is what our Lord took upon Himself, 'that through death he

might destroy him that had the power of death, that
is, the devil; and deliver them, who through fear of
death were all their lifetime subject to bondage.' 'Thou
shalt not' is the beginning of wisdom. But the end of
wisdom, the new law, is 'Thou shalt.' To be Christian is
to be old? Not a bit of it. To be Christian is to be
reborn, and free, and unafraid, and immortally young."

Smoke on the Mountain, © 1954, Westminster Press, p. 20.

Henri J. M. Nouwen:
Model Christ's Radical Love

"After washing His disciples' feet, Jesus says, 'I have
given you an example so that you may copy what I
have done to you' (John 13:15). After giving Himself as
food and drink, He says, 'Do this in remembrance of
me' (Luke 22:19). Jesus calls us to continue His mission
of revealing the perfect love of God in this world. He
calls us to total self-giving. He does not want us to
keep anything for ourselves. Rather, He wants our love
to be as full, as radical, and as complete as His own. He
wants us to bend ourselves to the ground and touch
the places in each other that most need washing. He

also wants us to say to each other, 'Eat of me and drink of me.' By this complete mutual nurturing, He wants us to become one body and one spirit, united by the love of God."

Show Me the Way, © 1995, Crossroad Publishing Company, pp. 130–1.

Billy Graham:
Be Salt and Light

"Jesus had the most open and all-encompassing mind that this world has ever seen. His own inner conviction was so strong, so firm, so unswerving that He could afford to mingle with any group secure in the knowledge that He would not be contaminated. It is fear that makes us unwilling to listen to another's point of view, fear that our own ideas may be attacked. Jesus had no such fear, no such pettiness of viewpoint, no need to fence Himself off for His own protection. He knew the difference between graciousness and compromise, and we would do well to learn from Him. He set for us the most magnificent and glowing example of truth combined with mercy of all time, and in departing said: 'Go ye and do likewise' (Luke 10:37)."

Unto the Hills, © 1986, Word Publishing, pp. 123–4.

quick quotes
wisdom past and present

Bob Briner:
Get Out of Your Christian Bubble

"We [Christians] have created a phenomenal sub-culture with our own media, entertainment, educational system, and political hierarchy so that we have the sense that we're doing a lot. But what we've really done is create a ghetto that is easily dismissed by the rest of society. . . . It's time for the lambs to roar. What I'm calling for is a radically different way of thinking about our world. Instead of running from it, we need to rush into it. And instead of just hanging around the fringes of our culture, we need to be right smack dab in the middle of it."

Roaring Lambs, © 1993, Zondervan Publishing House, pp. 29, 31.

Brennan Manning:
Show the World How to Trust

"The disciple living by grace rather than law has undergone a decisive conversion—a turning from mistrust to trust. The foremost characteristic of living by grace is trust in the redeeming work of Jesus Christ. To believe deeply, as Jesus did, that God is present and at

how to live your witness

work in human life is to understand that I am a beloved child of this Father and hence, free to trust. That makes a profound difference in the way I relate to myself and others; it makes an enormous difference in the way I live. To trust Abba, both in prayer and life, is to stand in childlike openness before a mystery of gracious love and acceptance."

The Ragamuffin Gospel, © 1990, Multnomah Books, p. 74.

C. S. Lewis:
Don't Be Afraid of Confrontation

"As Christians we are tempted to make unnecessary concessions to those outside the faith. We give in too much. Now, I don't mean that we should run the risk of making a nuisance of ourselves by witnessing at improper times, but there comes a time when we must show that we disagree. We must show our Christian colours, if we are to be true to Jesus Christ. We cannot remain silent or concede everything away."

God in the Dock, © 1970, William B. Eerdmans Publishing Company, p. 262.

wisdom

quick quotes

wisdom past and present

 J. I. Packer:

Let the Holy Spirit Testify through You

    "When Christ left the world, He committed His
cause to His disciples. He made them responsible for
going and making disciples of all the nations. 'But you
will receive power when the Holy Spirit comes on you;
and you will be my witnesses in Jerusalem, and in all
Judea and Samaria, and to the ends of the earth,' were
His parting words to them on Olivet, before He
ascended (Acts 1:8). Such was their appointed task. But
what sort of witnesses were they likely to prove? They
had never been good pupils; they had consistently failed
to understand Christ, and missed the point of His
teaching throughout His earthly ministry. . . . Was it not
morally certain that, with the best will in the world,
they would soon get the truth of the gospel inextrica-
bly mixed up with a mass of well-meant misconcep-
tions, and their witness would rapidly be reduced to a
twisted, garbled, hopeless muddle? The answer to this
question is no; because Christ sent the Holy Spirit to
them, to teach them all truth and so save them from all

error, to remind them of what they had been taught already, and to reveal to them the rest of what the Lord had meant for them to learn. 'But the Counselor, the Holy Spirit, whom the Father will send in my name, will teach you all things and will remind you of everything I have said to you' (John 14:26)."

Knowing God, © 1973, InterVarsity Press, p. 61.

Philip Yancey:
Strive to Be Like God

"We want God to be like us: tangible, material, perceptible (hence the long history of idolatry). We want God to speak in audible words that we can clearly understand (Ezra Stiles of Yale studied Hebrew in order to converse with God in His native language!). Apart from the Incarnation and rare epiphanies, however, God shows little interest in corresponding on our level. God has, in the common phrase 'been there, done that,' and has no reason to confine Himself to time and space any longer than necessary. Rather, God seeks from us correspondence in a spiritual realm and seems more interested in other kinds of growth: justice, mercy, peace, grace, and love—spiritual qualities that can work themselves out in a material world. In short, God wants us to be more like Him."

Reaching for the Invisible God, © 2000,
Zondervan Publishing House, pp. 109–10.

Madeleine L'Engle:
Help Them See the God of Wonders

"The Virgin Birth has never been a major stumbling block in my struggle with Christianity; it's far less mind-boggling than the power of all creation stooping so low as to become one of us. But I find myself disturbed at the changing, by some committee or other, of the 'myth' that brought God and the human creature together in marvelous at-one-ment, as Jacob's ladder brought heaven and earth together. That's the wonder that God can reach out and become one with that which has been created."

A Stone for a Pillow, © 1986, Harold Shaw Publishers, pp. 107–8.

Max Lucado:
Help Them See Jesus

"Only in seeing his Maker does a man truly become man. For in seeing his Creator man catches a glimpse of what he was intended to be. He who would see his God would then see the reason for death and the purpose of time. Destiny? Tomorrow? Truth? All are questions within the reach of the man who knows his source. It is in seeing Jesus that man sees his Source."

God Came Near, © 1987, Multnomah Books, p. 96.

Mother Teresa:
Be the Living Expression of God's Kindness

"Spread love everywhere you go: First of all, in your own house. Give love to your children, to your wife or husband, to a next-door neighbor. . . . Let no one ever come to you without leaving better and happier. Be the living expression of God's kindness; kindness in your face, kindness in your eyes, kindness in your smile, kindness in your warm greeting."

Your Bridge to a Better Future, © 1997 by John C. Maxwell,
Thomas Nelson Publishers, p. 77.

John Eldredge:
Quench Their Desire for God

"We've been told that desire is the enemy. After all, desire is the single major hindrance to the goal—

how to live your witness

quick quotes
wisdom past and present

getting us in line. And so, we are told to kill desire, and call it sanctification. But God is not the enemy of desire. 'Delight yourself also in the Lord,' the psalmist tells us, 'and he shall give you the desires of your heart' (Psalm 37:4 NKJV). God is the One who made these deep hearts within us, created us as men and women with these deep longings. And though we turned our backs on Him, He pursued us, called us back to His own good heart and intends to bring us life again. This is why holiness is not deadness; it is passion. It is being more attuned to our desires, to what we were truly made for and therefore what we really want."

Dare to Desire, © 2002, J. Countryman, pp. 74–75.

Oswald Chambers:
Be Your Brother's Keeper

quote

"Has it ever dawned on you that you are responsible for other souls spiritually before God? For instance, if I allow any private deflection from God in my life, everyone about me suffers. . . . When once you allow physical selfishness, mental slovenliness, moral obtuseness, spiritual density, everyone belonging to your crowd will suffer. 'But,' you say, 'who is sufficient for these things if you erect a standard like that?' Our sufficiency is of God, and of Him alone."

My Utmost for His Highest, © 1935, Dodd, Mead & Company, p. 46.

Dietrich Bonhoeffer:
Help Them Count the Cost

"Costly grace is the gospel, which must be sought again and again, the gift that must be asked for, the door at which a man must knock. Such grace is costly because it calls us to follow, and it is grace because it calls us to follow Jesus Christ. It is costly because it costs a man his life, and it is grace because it gives a man the only true life. It is costly because it condemns sin, and grace because it justifies the sinner. Above all, it is costly because it cost God the life of His Son: "ye were bought at a price," and what has cost God much cannot be cheap for us. Above all, it is grace because God did not reckon His Son too dear a price to pay for our life, but delivered Him up for us. Costly grace is the Incarnation of God."

The Cost of Discipleship, © 1959, Collier Books, pp. 47–9.

quick quotes
wisdom past and present

quote

Charles H. Spurgeon:
Witness with Confidence

"Let us go forward into the unknown future, linked eternally with Jesus. If the men of the world should cry, 'Who is this that cometh up from the wilderness, leaning upon her beloved?' (Song of Solomon 8:5 KJV) we will joyfully confess that we do lean on Jesus and that we mean to lean on Him more and more. Our faithful God is an ever-flowing well of delight, and our fellowship with the Son of God is a full river of joy. Knowing these glorious things, we cannot be discouraged."

All of Grace, © 1992, Moody Press, p. 125.

quote

Elisabeth Elliot:
Freely Give What You Cannot Keep

"Committing themselves and all their carefully laid plans to Him who had so unmistakably brought them thus far, they waited for the Aucas [Indians in Ecuador]. Before 4:30 that afternoon, the quiet waters of the Curaray flowed over the bodies of the five comrades, slain by the men they had come to win for Christ, whose banner they had borne. The world

quick quotes
wisdom past and present

called it a nightmare of tragedy. The world did not recognize the truth of the second clause in Jim Elliot's
credo: 'He is no fool who gives what he cannot keep to
gain what he cannot lose.' "

Shadow of the Almighty, © 1958, Harper & Row Publishers, pp. 18–19.

Jesus Christ:
Be My Hands and Feet

"The King will reply, 'I tell you the truth,
whatever you did for one of the least of these broth-
ers of mine, you did for me.' Then he will say to
those on his left, 'Depart from me, you who are
cursed, into the eternal fire prepared for the devil
and his angels. For I was hungry and you gave me
nothing to eat, I was thirsty and you gave me noth-
ing to drink. I was a stranger and you did not
invite me in, I needed clothes and you did not
clothe me, I was sick and in prison and you did
not look after me.' They also will answer, 'Lord,
when did we see you hungry or thirsty or a stranger
or needing clothes or sick or in prison, and did not

quick quotes
wisdom past and present

*help you?' He will reply, 'I tell you the truth, what-
ever you did not do for one of the least of these, you
did not do for me.' Then they will go away to eternal punishment, but the righteous to eternal life."*

—Matthew 25:40–46

know what you believe

You step through the front doors of your school, make your way down a long, crowded corridor lined with hundreds of lockers and spot the one assigned to you. Just before you twist the dial, you glance over both shoulders. . .and pause.

> *This is crazy. . .I just can't do it.*
> *There are way too many people around!*
> *Why did I ever make such a stupid pact?*
> *It'll be social suicide for sure!*
> *Will I be breaking a rule?*
> *What if I get kicked outta school?*

You swallow hard and groan—trying desperately to push all the wild thoughts out of your head. Then you do something radical, something you insisted you'd never do. You kneel in front of your locker and begin to pray. But less than one second into your conversation with God, you feel someone brush against you.

You open your eyes and gasp!

It's your best friend—the one from church who talked you into making this prayer pact. He's accompanied by his girlfriend. The two of them are kneeling by you—praying!

> *This isn't so bad.*
> *Yeah, people are staring. . .but I can handle this.*

Actually, it's pretty cool.
I have a good feeling about this school year.
It's gonna be different. Way different!

FACT:

Nearly 6 billion people inhabit this planet. It's estimated that more than 4.1 billion of them don't know Christ.

FACT:

Of the nearly 2 billion people who claim to be Christians, fewer than half pray or read their Bibles daily.

FACT:

While more than 80 percent of North American evangelicals say they believe in the authority of the Bible, more than 50 percent of them also believe that "absolute truth does not exist."

Do these facts disturb you? Do they make you want to stand up and do something? We hope so.

It's time for a revolution—a spiritual revolution. Today, more than ever, this planet needs a true counterculture. We need a "back to truth" movement so we can have a real "back to the Bible" movement. And if ever there was a group designed for such a task, that group is formed by young people who follow Christ.

Before Jesus ascended into heaven, He gave you a big job: "Go into all the world and preach the Good News to all creation" (Mark 16:15). He also gave you a bunch of assuring promises, including these three:

- "You will receive power when the Holy Spirit comes on you" (Acts 1:8).

- "The one who is in you is greater than the one who is in the world" (1 John 4:4).

- "Surely I am with you always, to the very end of the age" (Matthew 28:20).

Imagine that—the God of the universe forgives your sins, promises you eternal life with Him, then gives you the power and authority to fulfill His work on earth. (He even stays with you every step of the way!)

But you won't be effective for God if you stay in a safe comfort zone and hide your faith from the world. You also won't be able to speak up if you don't know the basics of what you believe.

On the pages that follow, we arm you with some foundations of the Christian faith so you can proclaim the Gospel with confidence.

Christianity at a glance

God

There's only one. "You alone are the Lord. You made the heavens, even the highest heavens, and all their starry host, the earth and all that is on it, the seas and all that is in them. You give life to everything, and the multitudes of heaven worship you" (Nehemiah 9:6).

Jesus Christ

He's fully God. "I am the light of the world. Whoever follows me will never walk in darkness, but will have the light of life" (John 8:12).

Holy Spirit

Believers are empowered by a holy He, not a holy it. "I will not leave you as orphans; I will come to you" (John 14:18).

The Enemy

He is the destroyer of souls. "Be self-controlled and alert. Your enemy the devil prowls around like a roaring lion looking for someone to devour" (1 Peter 5:8).

Man and Sin

We live in a fallen world and are flawed by sin. "For all have sinned and fall short of the glory of God" (Romans 3:23).

Salvation

God promises eternal life to all who follow Him. "I give them eternal life, and they shall never perish; no one can snatch them out of my Father's hand" (John 10:28–29).

Holy Bible

The Bible is the Word of God, as well as our roadmap for life. "All Scripture is God-breathed and is useful for teaching, rebuking, correcting and training in righteousness, so that the man of God may be thoroughly equipped for every good work" (2 Timothy 3:16–17).

God

God is the infinite, holy Creator of the universe who has always existed, and who created the universe by the power of His Word (Hebrews 11:3). In Exodus 3:14, God told Moses, "I am who I am." There is only one true God (Isaiah 45:5).

In his book, *Knowing God,* author J. I. Packer describes five basic truths about God:[8]

▶ **God has spoken to man,** and the Bible is His Word, given to us to teach us about salvation and to make us wise in His ways.

▶ **God is Lord and King over His world;** He rules all things for His own glory, displaying His perfections in all that He does, in order that men and angels may worship and adore Him.

▶ **God is our Savior,** active in sovereign love through the Lord Jesus Christ to rescue believers from the guilt and power of sin, to adopt them as His sons, and to bless them accordingly.

- **God is Triune;** there are within the Godhead three persons, the Father, the Son, and the Holy Ghost; and the work of salvation is one in which all three act together—the Father purposing redemption, the Son securing it, and the Spirit applying it.

- **Godliness means responding to God's revelation**—in trust and obedience, faith and worship, prayer and praise, submission and service. Life must be seen and lived in the light of God's Word. This, and nothing else, is true religion.

Jesus Christ

Jesus is the only begotton Son of God, yet completely God and one with the Father (John 10:30). Jesus is the mediator between God and humankind, having been sent by God to earth to die for us and to forgive our sins (John 1:29). Here are some attributes of Jesus:

No sin.

The Bible stamps the words "no sin" on the person of Christ three times:

- God made him who had no sin to be sin for us, so that in him we might become the righteousness of God (2 Corinthians 5:21).

- He committed no sin, and no deceit was found in his mouth (1 Peter 2:22).

- But you know that he appeared so that he might take away our sins. And in him is no sin (1 John 3:5).

Christ had to be without sin to qualify as the perfect sacrifice for the sin of mankind—the perfect sacrifice for your sin. As God's sinless sacrifice, Jesus made it possible for you to trust Him and be forgiven.

Jesus is present in another sense: the Bible.

If you look carefully enough, you'll find Jesus on every page. Think of Isaac on the altar, his life saved by a sacrificial ram (Genesis 22). Jesus is all over that story. The written Word is Christ, the Living Word, in book form. You can't say Jesus is "not around" if you've got a Bible sitting on your dresser.

Holy Spirit

The Holy Spirit is the third person of the Godhead, who has always existed with God the Father and Jesus Christ.

"For we were all baptized by one Spirit into one body—whether Jews or Greeks, slave or free—and we were all given the one Spirit to drink" (1 Corinthians 12:13). Not only does the Holy Spirit baptize every believer into the body of Christ (the Church), He also gives each of us spiritual gifts and empowers us to live godly lives (see Galatians 5:22–23).

the enemy

We're all targets of the evil one. Satan wants to lure us into a hostile position toward God, and his biggest ally is our flesh itself, which is the human, physical dimension of our life that instinctively wants to live independently from God. Even though we now have a new nature in Christ, the sinful world still tempts us to return to those old ways of thinking and living. (See Romans 8:5–8 and Ephesians 2:3.)

So, how can we survive? The answer is basic, but vital—and one you'll find repeated in this book: Have a personal, active relationship with Jesus Christ. The Lord is your ultimate ally—your ultimate defender.

▸ **Know the enemy's tactics.** Satan knows just which buttons to push to tempt you away from depending on Christ. He has watched your behavior over the years and knows where your are weak. That's where he attacks.

▸ **Choose your weapons.** While you can't outsmart or outmuscle the flesh or the devil on your own, you can gain victory in your daily struggle against sin. The Lord has armed every Christian with spiritual weapons packed with "divine power": (1) the Sword of the Spirit—the Holy Bible—and (2) prayer. Colossians 3:16 tells Christians to let "the word of Christ richly dwell within you," and Philippians 4:7 promises that "the peace of God. . .shall guard your hearts and your minds in Christ Jesus."

man and sin

At this point in your life, the whole issue of dying is probably the furthest thing from your mind. But stop for a moment and ask yourself a few questions: "If I died tomorrow, would I go to heaven?" "Is death the end?"

If you have a personal relationship with Jesus Christ, then the answers to these questions is, "Yes, I will spend eternity with God in heaven. Death is not the end."

Despite the fact that we "all have sinned and fall short of the glory of God" (Romans 3:23)—and even though sin leads to death—God has given us eternal life through Jesus (see Romans 6:23).

salvation

Mankind is saved from sin and death by believing in and following Jesus Christ (John 3:16). There's nothing we can do to earn our salvation; it is God's gracious gift to us (Ephesians 2:8, 10).

In his book, *A Gift of Love,* author Charles Stanley explains salvation this way: "God sent His Son, Jesus Christ, to earth to reestablish the personal line of communication that was severed by the Fall. Salvation is the first step we take toward knowing the intimate side of God's love."[7]

God doesn't want anyone to miss out on eternal life with

Him. But the bottom line is this: Those who don't have a personal friendship with Jesus—those who don't repent of their sins and accept Christ in their hearts—will not have eternal life with God. That's why it's important to share the Lord's plan of salvation with everyone.

the holy Bible

All Scripture is "God-breathed" and offers solid advice for just about every situation you'll ever encounter. Through the Word, God teaches, rebukes, corrects and trains us in righteousness. Without the Bible, we wouldn't know: (a) what God is like, (b) His plan for humans like you and me, (c) how much He loves us, (d) the right way to live on this planet, or (e) anything about what will happen to us after death.

God's word is timeless and accurate in everything He felt was essential for us to know. There are no discrepancies in His promises, commands, and warnings.

know your Rights

The Constitutions of both the United States and Canada protect your freedom of religious expression. Do you know what you can and can't do on a public school campus? Take our quiz and find out.

Students can pray on a public school campus.

[ ] YES   [ ] NO

Students can read their Bibles on a public school campus.

[ ] YES   [ ] NO

Students can form religious clubs on campus if other extracurricular clubs exist.

[ ] YES   [ ] NO

Students can hand out tracts, flyers, or other religious materials on campus.

[ ] YES   [ ] NO

Rights
Rights

Students can do research papers, speeches, and so forth, with religious themes.

[ ] YES   [ ] NO

Students can be exempt from participating in assignments that are contrary to their religious beliefs.

[ ] YES   [ ] NO

Students can discuss religious issues although other students may overhear them.

[ ] YES   [ ] NO

Guess what?

The answer to all of the above questions is YES!

students' bill of rights

on a

public school campus

1. THE RIGHT to meet with other religious students.

The Equal Access Act allows students the freedom to meet on campus for the purpose of discussing religious issues.

2. THE RIGHT to identify your religious beliefs through signs and symbols.

Students are free to express their religious beliefs through signs and symbols.

3. THE RIGHT to talk about your religious beliefs on campus.

Freedom of speech is a fundamental right mandated in the Constitution and does not exclude the school yard.

4. THE RIGHT to distribute religious literature on campus.

Distributing literature on campus may not be restricted simply because it religious.

5. THE RIGHT to pray on campus.

Students may pray alone or with others so long as it does not disrupt school activities or is not forced on others.

6. THE RIGHT to carry or study your Bible on campus.

The Supreme Court of the United States has said that only state directed Bible reading is unconstitutional.

7. THE RIGHT to do research papers, speeches, and creative projects with religious themes.

The First Amendment to the U.S. Constitution does not forbid all mention of religion in public schools.

8. THE RIGHT to be exempt.

Students may be exempt from activities and class content that contradict their religious beliefs.

9. THE RIGHT to celebrate or study religious holidays on campus.

Music, art, literature, and drama that have religious themes are permitted as part of the curriculum for school activities if presented in an objective manner as a traditional part of the cultural and religious heritage of the particular holiday.

10. THE RIGHT to meet with school officials.

The First Amendment forbids Congress to make any law that would restrict the right of the people to petition the government (school officials).

real-life
s t o r y

a new heart, a new faith

Today, Dan Krainert is a solid man of God with a strong heart for evangelism. (In fact, he operates a successful Christian outreach from his home in California.) But during his teen years in the late 80s, Dan wasn't sure what he believed. That is, until a dangerous heart condition nearly ended his life. Here's Dan's story.

Death? At age 17? Dan Krainert couldn't believe what his doctor was telling him. Suddenly he felt cold and empty. Every muscle seemed to tremble. Staring out the window, he tried to blink away the tears. "Just tell me how long I've got."

"At the very best, a year, if no further action is taken."

"Further action?" Dan's father blurted. "We've already done everything. Everything!"

Dr Strunk stroked his beard. "Let me rephrase that. If no more advanced action is taken."

"What are you suggesting, Doctor? What else can we do for our son?" Mr. Krainert's jaw was trembling visibly.

"I'd like you to consider a heart transplant. . .it's a last resort."

"And without it?" Dan asked.

"Like I said, its' just a matter of months." Dr Strunk looked straight into Dan's eyes. "I'm afraid we've reached the point where nothing else can be done."

More than twenty years ago, a sandy-haired teen from Napa, California, desperately needed a new heart. Dan Krainert had an incurable disease that was destroyed his vital organ. Time was running out.

When Dan was only six weeks old, his mother rushed him to the hospital and insisted that doctors examine him from head to toe. She knew something was wrong. He appeared sick and undernourished.

Physicians discovered congestive cardiomyopathy with secondary mitral regurgitation—a bad heart with a leaky valve. Predicting that Dan wouldn't live to see his first birthday, they promptly started him on an assortment of strong drugs, hoping to prolong his life.

But to everyone's surprise, the drugs allowed Dan to develop as any kid would. In the years that followed, he gained weight and even surpassed the size of other youngsters in his class. When Dan was eleven, the doctors decided they had misdiagnosed his condition and took him off the pills.

Dan developed into a muscular, hard-hitting baseball player in tenth grade, and a musically and dramatically inclined eleventh-grader, bursting with life—until his seventeenth birthday.

On a June night—a sticky summer evening in California—Dan couldn't sleep. He tossed and turned, then bolted upright. An odd pain began in his throat and slowly spread throughout his body. His jaw tightened, his teeth clenched. It was difficult to utter a sound. The back of his neck tensed, and pain shot down the underside of his arms and across his chest. His lungs felt squeezed together, and he couldn't catch his breath.

"Dear God, please!" he gasped, trying to massage the fire from his chest. Fighting off the sheets, he fumbled for his glasses and stumbled to the door. His parents burst in, faces ashen.

"Where does it hurt?" his mother asked, putting her arm around him.

Dan motioned to his chest. "It's not indigestion, and it's no hernia. The pain is in my heart!"

His parents helped him to the couch and eased him back onto the cushions.

"No!" Dan yelled. "I've got to sit up. It's worse lying down. I. . .I think I'm dying!"

"Libby, call the doctor!" his dad ordered.

Doctors discovered that the heart disease, which had remained in remission all those years, had resumed its fatal course. During the following year, he had six heart failures (when the heart doesn't pump efficiently) and two cardiac arrests (when the heart stops beating).

"It was difficult, especially at that age," says Dan, a soft-spoken young man. "I was scared."

After the wave of heart disorders, Dan wrestled with the doctor's grim news. A heart transplant didn't guarantee life. It meant continued suffering. And after all of the pain and tears, his body could still reject the heart.

Then he thought about a question he had heard the summer before during a televised Billy Graham crusade: "Do you have eternal life?"

"Billy's words stirred my spirit," Dan says. "But when I asked myself: If I died tomorrow, would I go to heaven? I honestly didn't know."

Dan says he knew God existed, "but it never appeared that way in my church." He would tag along each Sunday morning with his parents, but "the place seemed pretty empty even when it was full. The minister always sounded like he was reciting from an encyclopedia." God seemed far away.

That night was different, though. Dan knew a little about suffering, and "Billy Graham made sense," he says.

"I bought a Bible and found out I should be changing a few things. I discovered that you have to make a commitment to Christ while you can."

By the time the doctor urged him to consider a transplant, Dan had settled the matter of eternal life.

"When all this started happening, I prayed a lot

because I wanted to know God's will about whether or not to have the transplant," he says. "I knew He could heal me with or without the surgery if He wanted to.

"I read Philippians 4:6–7: 'Do not be anxious about anything, but in everything, by prayer and petition, with thanksgiving, present your requests to God. And the peace of God, which transcends all understanding, will guard your hearts and your minds in Christ Jesus.'

"Only if you depend on God's Word and give everything to Him—your hurts, your fears, your trust, your life—will you find peace. When I did this, the doors opened for me to have that transplant."

Dan applied for a transplant at Stanford University. "You have to be sick enough to need a transplant, but well enough to survive one," he says. "You also have to have a reason and will to live—and I did. I explained to the doctors that I didn't believe that it was the Lord's will for me to die just yet. I believed that He was going to let me live and then use me to be His witness."

He was accepted and began the long wait for an available heart, one with the same blood and tissue type as his.

"The physicians explained that just because I needed a new heart didn't mean I could get one," Dan says. "They told me four hundred people a year apply, and only one in ten get one. Of those who are accepted as transplant patients, many die just waiting for a heart to become available."

Dan beat the odds. On December 22, 1980, he received the heart of a nineteen-year-old marine who had just been killed in a motorcycle accident.

"You know what I thought about when I was waiting for a heart?" Dan says. "I thought, *Somebody out there is going to die, and I don't know who it is, and I can't do anything about it.* You feel kind of selfish, hoping for it to happen.

"Then I though about Jesus Christ and the price He paid," Dan adds. "He gave me a new heart so I could live eternally.

"The marine didn't know that would be the last day of his life. And, like him, you could be killed on the freeway. I think everyone should ask himself, 'If I died today, or if Christ came today, would I be ready to meet Him?' You have to trust Christ today, not tomorrow. Otherwise it could be too late."

The heart had been removed from the young marine's body and flown to Stanford. Dan's diseased heart was removed and the new heart trimmed to fit and sutured into place—all within two hours and twenty-seven minutes. (The process usually takes five to twelve hours.)

When Dan awoke the next morning, tubes protruded from his nose and chest. A room full of high-tech equipment monitored each breath.

Dan was groggy but glad: He would live—today, tomorrow, and through Christ, forever. Yet the days that followed were laced with frustration. Pain flared from his sternum.

"You're isolated in a room that's sterile," he says. "You can't have too many visitors, and everybody who comes in has to wear a mask and gown. All you can see is their eyes."

But through the pain and spaced out sensation of the drugs, Dan noticed something else. "Before the operation, I was gasping for each breath, as if a football player were standing on my chest. Now I was breathing without fighting.

"Before, I had been conscious of my heartbeat; I could always feel it, pounding erratically. Now, I couldn't feel my heart. The one sensation I did feel—the hurt of the incision—was a good pain, a pain that was going to give me healing."

Can I possibly handle my senior year? Dan asked himself, thinking about the work he had to make up. And when he returned to school that fall, "there was a separation from other students. It was as if they were curious wanting to talk, but afraid to."

Then on a rainy September day in 1981, ten months after the transplant, Dan's mom hung up the phone and covered her face with her hands.

"Mom, what's wrong?" Dan asked.

"Stanford just called," she said blankly. "You're in rejection."

"You're kidding." Dan paused to consider the implications. "So what do I do now?"

"More medicine. . .higher doses."

Dan already felt like a walking medicine cabinet—he took more than thirty pills every day. Now he would have to remember to take a daily dose of prednisone.

"Do you know what that will mean to me?" he asked, agonizing over the familiar list of side effects: brittle bones, weakness, deteriorating muscles, bruising, bloating, nervousness.

He retreated to his room and began to question God. Didn't He care anymore?

Then Dan thought about the small group of Christians at his high school who met together every day and prayed that Dan would have courage and faith, that he would sense that God was in control. He thought about the heroes of faith mentioned in Hebrews 11:

"Others were tortured and refused to be released, so that they might gain a better resurrection. Some faced jeers and flogging, while still others were chained and put in prison. They were stoned; they were sawed in two; they were put to death by the sword. . . . These were all commended for their faith, yet none of them received what had been promised. God had planned something better for us so that only together with us would they be made perfect" (vv. 35-40).

Perhaps this trial would help him in some way. Perhaps it would help others.

"I realized that the Lord wanted to use me—sick, tired me," Dan says. "That's when my focus began to change from the fact that I was in rejection to the idea that I could grow through this, another ordeal. Good came out of it."

Asked how he held up during all his trials, Dan takes off his glasses and rubs his eyes, then smiles. "From the very beginning of these experiences nine years ago, I've realized that it has opened up so many opportunities to testify about how God has brought me out of them.

"I realized one thing right away, that when you become a Christian you're not immune to adversity. There are too many Christians—who have been Christians for a long time—who get very surprised by adversity, as if God is not with them because something has happened to them," Dan says. "But they are missing the point.

"Christians will face the same trials non-Christians go through. The difference is that they have a living God who acts on their behalf. In this way, the world can recognize God through His works in the believer's life. He is

recognized through answers to prayer, restoration, healing. . .and through all of the other ways in which He
takes care of His children. I learned this from the very
beginning, and that is why my faith is still intact.

"As long as you know God, you can have peace,
knowing that He will protect you," Dan says. "I have
always known that I would come through my trials, and
that God will honor my faith in Him. So I look at each
experience as a new opportunity to be His witness."

At every opportunity, Dan tells people he is alive
by the grace and help of God, and urges everyone to
live each moment "as if it were a gift from God."

Today, he operates Praise Filled Ministries, an
outreach that prays for the sick and visits them in
area hospitals.

"There are so many people out there who get
shaken up by all the little things that happen. Sometimes it's harder to trust that God will see you
through those minor occurrences," Dan says. "It's
often easier to trust that the Lord will get you
through the big trials. But small or large, God still
wants us to trust Him.

"If Christ hadn't been willing to suffer or die on
the cross, there'd be no hope for us. But He trusted
His soul to His faithful Father, and He knew He was
doing what was right. In the same way, if I wasn't willing to suffer for the will of God, His purpose for me
and my life wouldn't be fulfilled."

Despite the trials, Dan has enjoyed more than twenty years of life that have been a gift from God. He says he wouldn't think of giving up.

"Every time I see my mom and dad, I get a sense of joy, of keeping hold of something precious. Every time I take a deep breath, every time I throw a baseball, every time I look at the green rolling hills surrounding Napa, I thank God for another day of life."

crash course on false religions

Every man, woman, and child in every corner of planet earth desperately wants to fill a God-sized void in their lives—whether they realize it or not. The fact is, we're all searching for truth and yearn to understand who we are and why we're here. We hunger for meaning and love and significance, and want to believe in something (or someone) bigger than ourselves—even if this quest takes us down some empty paths.

In India, for example, there are those who sleep on a bed of nails, hoping to become less earthy and more spiritual. *Ouch!* In the Middle East, many pray five times a day. *Too bad they don't always connect with the One, true God of the universe.* In Asia, truth seekers meditate to "purify the mind," while in Africa, some tribal customs demand the sacrifice of chickens and goats. *Wouldn't it be awesome if these people heard about the only sacrifice that can save a soul?*

People in the West are just as lost. In our fast-paced culture of high-tech toys and low-tech values, science is great at answering the *what* and *how* questions we encounter in life. But it can't answer the really big questions of *who* and *why*. That's where you come in. As a Christian, you're plugged in to absolute truth—the very truth the world seeks. You have a relationship with our Creator. . .the one and only God who forgives sins and offers eternal life. Yet how do you communicate absolute truth with someone who is blinded by a cult or a false world religion?

Check out this scenario. (It just might hit home.)

◆　　　　◆　　　　◆　　　　◆

It's a lazy Saturday afternoon, and you're kicking back on the couch when you hear a knock at the front door. Squinting out the peephole, you notice two men wearing ties and holding briefcases.

Ugh—salesmen. Or possibly computer geeks, you tell yourself. But you twist the doorknob anyway and greet them.

"Good afternoon," a man says with a big smile. "We're from a new church in your neighborhood. . .and were wondering if we could talk to you about God?"

You flash an equally big smile. "Oh, hey—that's cool," you say, "but I'm a Christian, and I'm already plugged into a great church. You may want to talk with someone on the block who doesn't know Jesus."

Ignoring you, the other guy standing on your porch pulls a pamphlet out of his briefcase—something with the word *tower* printed on the cover. He hands it to you, then says, "We'd like to introduce you to more than just a 'little god.' We're here to share the truth with you."

Truth?! Little God?! You tell yourself. *OK, something is really strange here.* Suddenly, your mind races back to a lesson you'd heard on cults at a youth group meeting, but you struggle to remember anything. *I think they're part of that church down the road, but I'm not sure. What do I say? Do I slam the door in their faces, or do I attempt to share what I believe? And even though these guys are really nice—will they actually listen to me?*

swimming in a sea of fake faith

The Bible warns that misguided people will try to lead us away from God: "I am astonished that you are so quickly deserting the one who called you by the grace of Christ and are turning to a different gospel—which is really no gospel at all. Evidently some people are throwing you into confusion and are trying to pervert the gospel of Christ" (Galatians 1:6–7).

Maybe you've already encountered members of a cult in your own neighborhood—or someone at school who's following a false world religion. Do you find yourself tongue-tied. . .and clueless about how to articulate your beliefs? Of course, you want a non-Christian to open his eyes to the truth, turn away from his sins, and accept Jesus Christ as Lord and Savior, which, in this case, requires changing religions. But how do you reach out?

Step No. 1:
Be confident about what you believe.

It's important to plug into God's Word so that when it's time to speak up, you won't be left mumbling, "Uh, ummm, I dunno, God is love, I guess."

The truth is, you need divine intervention—*every day!* In order to be an effective witness, you need to know what you believe, believe what you know, then live what you know and believe. Let us explain:

Know it! Get plugged in to the truth by getting grounded in what you believe. You can't share with others what you don't know.

Believe it! Stand firm in what you know. You can't convince others of something you doubt.

Live it! Consistently practice what you know and *believe.* You may have heard other Christians say stuff like, "Preach the gospel, and when necessary, use words."

Step No. 2:
Know how to spot a counterfeit faith.

Some cults and false religions resemble Christianity. That's why you need to know the red flags—the clues that warn you when a person's faith or belief system stands in opposition to God. (See "What Makes Christianity Different?" on the following page.)

Step No. 3:
Learn what *they* believe.

Before you approach someone about his faith, go over

the basics of what he believes and understand how it differs from Christianity. Strive to avoid arguments. You could actually win a theological debate but lose the battle for your friend's salvation if you're arguing. A discussion about differences is one thing, but arguments tend to get emotional. You don't want to put your friend on the defensive. And most importantly? Simply share the difference Jesus Christ is making in your life. There's nothing more powerful than a personal testimony!

what makes
Christianity different?

Keep in mind that many cults and false world religions deny that Jesus is the only way to eternal life. Others swap Him for their own stunted version of Jesus, a sort of minigod or mega-nice guy. They create their own gospel and their own way to heaven. The problem is, the wrong Jesus can't save us from our sins.

In his book, *What's with the Dudes at the Door?* (© 1998, Bethany House Publishers), author Kevin Johnson explains it this way: "You can see the same basic thrust all across the spectrum of cults. They deny what makes the Christian faith unique: (1) Jesus saves, because (2) humans need saving. False faiths take away from the glory of Jesus

Christ, who alone deserves praise for salvation, and give at least some of it to people. Rarely do cults try to take all the honor from God and give it to human beings, but neither do they give God all the credit."

The world is filled with tons of cults and false belief systems. Here's a quick look at how some cultic beliefs differ from Christian ones.

Christianity teaches:	some false religions teach:
There is only one God.	There are many gods.
God has always been God.	Divinity can be attained.
Humans can become God's children.	Humans can become gods.
God saves through Jesus Christ.	People can save themselves.
Believers spend eternity in heaven.	Humans can be reincarnated.
God alone is worthy of worship.	People become objects of worship.

a checklist of counterfeit faiths

false world religions

Bahai	Buddhism
Confucianism	Hare Krishna
Hinduism	Islam
Islam—Taliban	Islam—Nation of Islam
Jainism	Judaism
Mysticism	Rastafarianism
Romani	Shinto
Sikhism	Taoism
Vedanta	Zoroastrianism

Cults

The Boston Church	Children of God
Christian Science	Mormonism
Jehovah's Witness	New Age
Scientology	Seventh Day Adventist
Theosophy	Transcendental Meditation
Unification Church	Unitarian Universalist Church
Unity Movement	The Way International

Secular Worldviews

Agnosticism

Atheism

Existentialism

Marxism/Communism

Modernism

Naturalism

Post-Modernism

Secular Humanism

Occult Practices

Astrology

Black Mass

Dowsing

Fremasonry

Magic: The Gathering

Necromancy

Ouija Board

Parapsychology

Rosicrucianism

Shamanism

Satanism

Tarot Cards

Vodun

Wicca

trip to the library

For a more detailed look at cults and false world religions, check out these books:

Why So Many Gods? by K. Etue (© 2002, Thomas Nelson, Inc.)

So What's the Difference? by Fritz Ridenour (© 2001, Regal Books)

Jesus Among Other Gods by Ravi Zacharias (© 2000, W Publishing Group)

What's with the Dudes at the Door? by Kevin Johnson (© 1998, Bethany House Publishers)

highlights of the Islam faith

Regarding God

Muslims: There is no God but Allah.

Christians: God is revealed in Scripture as Father, Son, and Holy Spirit, three persons who are co-eternally God.

"Go therefore and make disciples of all the nations, baptizing them in the name of the Father, Son, and Holy Spirit, teaching them to observe all that I commanded you; and lo, I am with you always, even to the end of the age."

MATTHEW 28:19–20

Regarding Jesus Christ

Muslims: Jesus was only a man, a prophet below Mohammed in importance, who did not die for man's sins.

Christians: Christ is the Son of God, the sinless Redeemer who died and rose again for sinful man.

"For Christ also died for sins once for all, the just for the unjust, in order that he might bring us to God, having been put to death in the flesh, but made alive in the spirit."

1 PETER 3:18

Regarding Sin and Salvation

Muslims: Humans are born with hearts that are clean slates. If they commit sins, these can be overcome by acts of the will.

Christians: Men and women are born corrupted by sin, separated from God. Therefore, God sent his Son Jesus to die for our sins and to give us eternal life. The Cross is the center of God's redemptive plan. The crucifixion of Christ was prophesied in the Old Testament. Eyewitness accounts of that crucifixion are contained in each of the four Gospels.

"But God demonstrates his own love toward us, in that while we were yet sinners, Christ died for us."

ROMANS 5:12

(For more information on the Cross, see 1 Corinthians 1:23, 2:2, 15:3–4; Galatians 2:20, 6:12; Ephesians 2:16).

Six Doctrines of Islam[9]

Muslims are required to follow these six core beliefs:

1. **God.** There is only one true God, and his name is Allah. Allah is all-seeing, all-knowing and all-powerful.

2. **Angels.** The chief angel is Gabriel, who is said to have appeared to Muhammad. There is also a fallen angel named Shaitan (from the Hebrew "Satan"), as well as the followers of Shaitan, the jinns (demons).

3. **Scripture.** Muslims believe in four God-inspired books: the

Torah of Moses (what Christians call the Pentateuch—Genesis, Exodus, Leviticus, Numbers, and Deuteronomy), the Zabur (Psalms of David), the Injil (Gospel) of Jesus and the Quran (Revelations to Muhammad, often called Koran). But because Muslims believe that Jews and Christians corrupted their Scriptures, the Quran is Allah's final word to mankind. It supersedes and overrules all previous writings.

4. Muhammad. The Quran lists twenty-eight prophets of Allah. These include Adam, Noah, Abraham, Moses, David, Jonah, and Jesus. To the Muslim, the last and greatest prophet is Muhammad.

5. The end times. On the "last day," the dead will be resurrected. Allah will be the judge, and each person will be sent to heaven or hell. Heaven is a place of sensual pleasure. Hell is for those who oppose Allah and his prophet Muhammad.

6. Predestination. Allah has determined what he pleases, and no one can change what he has decreed (also known as kismet, the doctrine of fate). From this doctrine comes the most common Islamic phrase, "If it is Allah's will."

highlights of hinduism

Regarding God and Jesus Christ

Hinduism: No belief in a personal, loving God, but in Brahma, a formless, abstract, eternal being without attributes. Hindus believe that Jesus is not God but just one of many incarnations, or avatars of Vishnu.

Christianity: Belief that God is an eternal, personal, spiritual being in three persons—Father, Son, and Holy Spirit (see Matthew 3:13–17, 28:19; 2 Corinthians 13:14). Jesus Christ is God as well as man—sinless—and He died for our redemption (see John 1:13–14; 1 Peter 2:24).

Regarding sin and salvation

Hinduism: Calls sin "utter illusion" and seeks deliverance from samsara, the endless cycle of death and rebirth, through union with Brahma. This is achieved through devotion, meditation, good works, and self-control.

Christianity: Belief that sin is prideful rebellion that leads to eternal separation from God after living only one life, not many (see Romans 3:23; Hebrews 9:27) and that salvation is gained only through repentance of sins and believing in the sacrificial death and resurrection of Jesus Christ (see Romans 3:24; 1 Corinthians 15:3).

highlights of buddhism

On Suffering:

Buddha said: "To live is to suffer." The reasons for suffering are ignorance and craving.

Bible says: The Bible agrees that suffering is everywhere and that a good deal of suffering is due to misplaced desire. But at the core, the Bible provides a very different explanation for suffering: The entire world groans and all men suffer because of sin (see Romans 8:18–23).

On Craving:

Buddha says: All desire is bad and has to be removed.

Bible says: While there are bad desires, there are also good ones. For example, we're encouraged to have great desire for God, His glory in our lives, and for His kingdom (see Psalm 27:4; Matthew 6:33).

On Getting Rid of Selfish Desire:

Buddha says: The only way to rid oneself of selfish desire is through self-effort. For centuries his followers have tried to follow the Eightfold Path, but many have found that "the heart is deceitful above all things" and will sabotage the best of human intentions (see Jeremiah 17:9).

Bible says: Without the help of God the only way to end desire is to die. But with God, we can become "new creatures" who die figuratively to selfish desires (see John 3:5; Galatians 2:20).

On God and Jesus Christ

Buddha says: Buddhists deny the existence of a personal God or say that God's existence is irrelevant. Christ was a good teacher but less important than Buddha.

Bible says: God is personal, omniscient, and omnipotent. Jesus is the unique Son of God who died for mankind's sin (see John 1:34; Romans 5:6–8).

On Sin and Salvation

Buddha says: Sin is the lust that arises in one's life. The way to rid one's self of it is to follow the Eightfold Path or call on savior gods for help.

Bible says: Our desires are disordered by sin, which separates us from God. Only Christ can remove our guilt from sin and restore us with God (see Acts 4:12; Romans 3:10, 23).

highlights of the new age

Channeling and Talking with the Dead

What it's all about: Some people claim that ancient seers (or wise men) communicate with them, using their minds and bodies. You've probably heard about these individuals on TV talk shows.

For example, a woman in Washington claims that a 35,000-year-old "spiritual" teacher named Ramtha speaks through her. Some folks pay hundreds of dollars to see performances by "channelers" like her. (Channeler is another term for what the Bible calls a medium.)

Why it's the wrong channel: This whole practice

involves one thing: demon possession. Those who channel are *not* dealing with friendly little "Yodas" or E.T.-type critters who want to help them have an awesome life. These spirits are evil and use any kind of deception and dirty trick they can to gain control. . .of a person's mind, body, and soul. A demon's goal is to separate men and women from God and to send them on a fast track straight to. . .you guessed it. . .eternal darkness (hell).

Demonic spirits always take more than they give. So tell your friends not to fool around with this stuff. Because once they invite a demon to lunch, there's a good chance it won't be leaving.

What the Bible says: "Let no one be found among you who. . .casts spells, or who is a medium or spiritist or who consults the dead. Anyone who does these things is detestable to the Lord" (Deuteronomy 18:10–12).

Reincarnation

What it's all about: People who buy this lie think that after death, each person returns to an endless series of lives as different people. So if you were a good guy in the past life, things are going to go better for you this time around. If you were a jerk the last time, you'll pay for it by coming back as a bottom-of-the-heap person. Most New-Agers want very much to believe this. They think it will give them another chance to live a better life or to make up for a sin they've committed.

Why it's a dead-end belief: Reincarnation is in direct opposition to the Bible. God makes it clear that we live just one life in our bodies, die, and are then judged by God. And the thing that Christians celebrate is that Jesus forgives our sins—regardless of what we've done—when we repent and commit our lives to Him. He is the One who helps us live joyfully every day. . .even in eternity.

What the Bible Says: "Man is destined to die once, and after that to face judgment" (Hebrews 9:27).

Crystals

What it's all about: Many New-Agers believe that clear quartz crystals are a symbol of coming into alignment with cosmic harmony. They think a clear quartz radiates with divine white light and by seeing, touching, wearing, using, or meditating with these crystals one can actually work with that light in a physical form and facilitate a person's growth of awareness.

Why crystals can't solve your problems: Think about it. Spiritual awareness attained through a rock? Sounds sorta silly, doesn't it? The idea that crystals can protect or heal you is simply a lie. Whether sewn into the seam of jeans or hung in a car, a crystal is just a cool-looking rock and doesn't have any kind of power. Some teens actually carry a crystal to school, hoping it will help them do better on a test. This is foolish.

There is no biblical reason to believe in a New Age idea of psychic energy pervading the universe. Though we do believe in demonic energy that can work through occult practices, there is no reasonable basis to hold that crystals have inherent properties that make them transmitters of demonic power.

The fact is, crystals are a part of God's creation, which He pronounced good at the time He made them. There is nothing inherently occultic or spiritually dangerous about crystals, and if a Christian is interested in or attracted to them, he or she should be able to pursue this in good conscience.

What the Bible Says: "If any of you lacks wisdom, he should ask God, who gives generously to all without finding fault, and it will be given to him" (James 1:5).

Horoscopes

What it's all about: These seemingly innocent bits of advice that appear in newspapers everyday are a form of astrology, which is rooted in the New Age movement. Astrology is viewed as one of the ways to "develop your consciousness and spirituality" and "establish a means of communication with your higher self."

Why it's a dose of bad news: According to the Bible, astrology is in the same league as channeling. . .and both are off-limits to Christians.

Humans don't have to look to the stars for answers about life or the future. We can look to the One who made them—God. The fact is, getting people to search creation for answers, rather than the Creator, is a deception of the devil. And according to the Word of God, horoscopes represent a doorway to a spiritual dimension that God forbids us to enter.

What the Bible Says: "They are prophesying to you false visions, divinations, idolatries and the delusions of their own minds" (Jeremiah 14:14).

Ouija Boards and Occult-Related Games

What it's all about: On the surface, they appear to be innocent games that offer harmless fun. They come in a variety of forms: Ouija boards, crystal balls, tarot cards, and games such as Kabala, E.S.P., Telepathy, or Dungeons and Dragons.

Why these are the devil's toys: Each of these games has roots in the occult. Understand that when your hands are on a Ouija board or when you cast spells during an episode of Dungeons and Dragons, you have turned your back on God and renounced Jesus Christ and His plan for you. Yes, each of these forms of entertainment are all tools of the occult and should definitely be avoided. Play with these "toys," and you are at the mercy of the demon spirits behind them.

Instead, spend time with God and seek Him. Through Jesus, you will find life and healing and the best party you've ever imagined.

Remember, there is only one God and one mediator between God and man—Jesus Christ.

What the Bible Says: "It is the Lord your God you must follow, and him you must revere. Keep his commands and obey him; serve him and hold fast to him. That prophet or dreamer must be put to death, because he preached rebellion against the Lord your God, who brought you out of Egypt and redeemed you from the land of slavery; he has tried to turn you from the way the Lord your

God commanded you to follow. You must purge the evil from among you" (Deuteronomy 13:4–5).

daily
devotionals/
journal

interacting with Christ

week one

combat phony faith

day 1
aliens among us

communicate

"I'm tired of phony Christians—people who wear crosses and religious T-shirts and who say they follow Jesus, but who act no different than unbelievers. They curse, put others down, and are generally very selfish. How can I be different? What's the key to truly walking my talk?"

Dear friends, I urge you, as aliens and strangers in the world, to abstain from sinful desires, which war against your soul. Live such good lives among the pagans that, though they accuse you of doing wrong, they may see your good deeds and glorify God on the day he visits us.

1 PETER 2:11–12

experience Him

Live as an alien—this is a crucial first step in combating a phony faith. A Christian's walk, talk, and mind-set simply cannot mirror the world. We're called to be different: "Do not conform any longer to the pattern of this world, but be transformed by the renewing of your mind" (Romans 12:2).

Of course, this is much easier said than done, right? After all, who in their right mind would dare to stand out from the crowd? Conformity is much safer.

Actually seventeen-year-old Nathanael, of Farmington, Minnesota, isn't afraid to be different. "I'm a believer who will stand up and say that there should be a noticeable difference between Christians and non-Christians," he says. "The Bible gives an explanation of how a sincere Christian should act."

And listen to Josh, sixteen, of New Carlisle, Ohio: "Living as an authentic Christian means always being conscious of others' feelings, never putting others down, and not worrying so much about being cool or fitting in with the crowd. Above all, true Christians must have the guts to stand up for their beliefs."

Take some advice from Nathanael and Josh. As a follower of Christ, you've been set apart from the world—and called to be different, out of the ordinary, *extraordinary.* Your values are not the same as the world in which you live. You're moving toward becoming more like the Savior and less a part of planet earth.

Here's how the Bible instructs you to live: "Be imitators of

God, therefore, as dearly loved children and live a life of love, just as Christ loved us and gave himself up for us as a fragrant offering and sacrifice to God" (Ephesians 5:1–2).

share Him

- Tell others the truth about who they are. Be one of the few who reminds friends of their strengths and abilities.

- Cut back on the cuts! Don't let a few "friendly" put-downs become a habit. Vow to be different.

- Defend your friends, especially when someone is talking badly behind their backs. Also, never give in to the gossip game.

- Point others to the One who will always tell them the truth.

interactive journal

- **1 Peter 3:8–15:** Based on this passage, list how your life is supposed to be different.

_____

_____

_____

_____

▶ In the space provided, jot down stumbling blocks in your
faith. (For example, fear of being rejected by your peers or
feeling distant from God.) Spend some time praying over
this list, asking God to help you overcome the things that
keep you from having a deeper walk with Christ.

_____

_____

_____

_____

_____

_____

_____

_____

_____

my prayer:

_____
_____
_____
_____
_____
_____

answered prayer:

_____
_____
_____
_____

someone to pray for:

_____
_____
_____
_____

day **2**

live without secrets

"I can't stand hypocrites—yet I'm guilty of being one. I know how to act like a Christian in public, but my private thoughts and habits are way off base. I don't want to blow my witness. How can I get my life on track?"

"There is nothing concealed that will not be disclosed, or hidden that will not be made known. What you have said in the dark will be heard in the daylight, and what you have whispered in the ear in the inner rooms will be proclaimed from the roofs."

LUKE 12:2–3

experience Him

Live without secrets—that's the second critical step to overcoming phoniness in your faith. In other words, strive to be transparent. Make sure that the person you are in private matches the person you are in public.

Above all, see to it that your public side is consistent with the attitudes, teachings, and commandments of God.

The fact is, everything you say, everything you do, every-place you go, every thought you think is known by the Lord. Nothing can be hidden from Him. So, when you find yourself drawn to an immoral act—anything that would cause you to keep secrets from others—don't do it. Instead, stop, consider the consequences, and pray. Jesus will intervene: "No temptation has seized you except what is common to man. And God is faithful; he will not let you be tempted beyond what you can bear. But when you are tempted, he will also provide a way out so that you can stand up under it" (1 Corinthians 10:13).

share Him

Understand that there are two types of people in the world: those whose problems are visible to everyone around them and those who attempt to carry around secrets. Sadly, way too many Christians try to live in the second category, which ultimately puts them in the first category—usually at a cost: broken trust, ruined credibility, labels like "hypocrite." Don't let a secret come back to bite you. Make a change now.

▶ Seek the counsel of a trustworthy Christian and find an accountability partner. As you talk honestly with another person, you'll probably discover that the things you think are your problems are just symptoms of a deeper heart problem. And God is faithful and willing to help. If you let Him, He'll transform your damaged heart.

Understand that there's no greater witness than a Christian who is open and vulnerable about his or her struggles. On the other hand, believers who act as if they don't have problems are the biggest stumbling blocks to unbelieving family and friends.

Never believe the lie that you can ever say something, do something, go somewhere, or think things that God—and possibly others—won't know about. People who believe in secrets are people who get into trouble.

interactive journal

Titus 2:11–12: How can living as if there are no secrets help you to say "No" to ungodliness and "Yes" to the things that will make your life strong and solid?

_____

_____

_____

_____

_____

_____

◆ In the space provided, jot down how the world may attempt to throw you off course.

_____

_____

_____

_____

_____

_____

◆ List some "hot buttons" in your life that the enemy may attempt to use to take control your life—or to ruin your witness. Pray over this list.

_____

_____

_____

_____

_____

_____

my prayer:

answered prayer:

someone to pray for:

day 3
ultimate love

"Have Christians forgotten how to love? It's sad when unbelievers view the church as angry, judgmental, and cliquish. The world is hurting for love. We of all people need to model it."

"A new commandment I give to you, that you love one another; as I have loved you, that you also love one another. By this all will know that you are My disciples, if you have love for one another."

JOHN 13:34–35 NKJV

experience Him

Notice how the Bible's standard of love is often different from the one Christians demonstrate to the world?

Take a look at how love is supposed to be expressed: "Love is patient, love is kind and is not jealous; love does not brag and is not arrogant, does not act unbecomingly; it does not seek its own, is not provoked, does not take into account a wrong suffered, does not rejoice in unrighteousness, but rejoices with the truth; bears all things, believes all things, hopes all things, endures all things. Love never fails" (1 Corinthians 13:4–8 NASB).

Is this the kind of love Christians are called to share? Actually, it is. And despite the fact that our sin nature often causes us to fall short, it doesn't mean that we should lose hope or not attempt to live by this standard. God loves us despite our flaws and shortcomings. He is secure in who He is. Therefore, He loves us unconditionally and without giving a second thought to our failures.

In his book *A Gift of Love,* Dr. Charles Stanley writes: "He knows that there will be times when we look and act very unholy. Our misguided actions do not erase or stop the love of God. Sin can separate us from His blessings and intimate fellowship, but there is never a time when God withholds His love."[10]

share Him

▶ Understand that our love for others is evidence of our love for God. And when we love others unconditionally—forgiving them and reaching out to them—we can approach Jesus confidently in prayer. It is our assurance that our prayers will be heard (see 1 John 5:14–15).

▶ Communicate ultimate love: "For God is love and He sent His Son to save us from our sin. Christ was the Lamb of God slain for us, who rose from the dead and now lives on the throne. Through His grace we know He will touch and heal our pain and give us strength to meet each day. With the shield of faith and the sword of the Word we will win the fight. Our foe will not beat us when we stand firm and true."

▶ Demonstrate ultimate love: Share the love you experience through Christ with your friends—just as Jesus "laid down His life for His friends" (see John 15:13). Let your speech and actions be a clear message of God's salvation and grace and love.

interactive journal

▶ **Psalm 139:8–10:** What does this passage tell you about God's love?

_____

_____

_____

_____

_____

_____

_____

2 Corinthians 1:3–11: Describe how our Lord is the "God of all comfort." Name some practical ways that we can follow His example and reach out to those who suffer.

_____

_____

_____

_____

_____

my prayer:

_____

_____

_____

_____

_____

_____

_____

answered prayer:

_____

_____

_____

_____

_____

someone to pray for:

_____

_____

_____

_____

_____

day **4**

choose integrity

"What is the Bible's definition of *integrity*, and how are we supposed to 'live it' in the world?"

communicate

> *For no one can lay any foundation other than the one already laid, which is Jesus Christ. If any man builds on this foundation using gold, silver, costly stones, wood, hay or straw, his work will be shown for what it is, because the Day will bring it to light. It will be revealed with fire, and the fire will test the quality of each man's work. If what he has built survives, he will receive his reward. If it is burned up, he will suffer loss; he himself will be saved, but only as one escaping through the flames.*
>
> 1 CORINTHIANS 3:11–15

experience Him

Jesus Christ lived His integrity all the way to the cross. And as the Scriptures tell us, the rewards for following His example on earth last forever in heaven. The fact is, we simply don't have much of a future without integrity. Proverbs 10:9 describes it this way: "The man of integrity walks securely."

Here are some other clues the Bible gives us about integrity:

- Integrity serves as a guide in life's moral decisions (Proverbs 11:3).

- Integrity hates falsehood in every form (Proverbs 13:5–6).

- Integrity is something to be held on to, even in tough times (Job 2:3).

- Integrity keeps its word even when it hurts (Psalm 15:1–4).

- Integrity isn't afraid to run when evil comes knocking (2 Timothy 2:22).

- Integrity says both *yes* and *no* and means what it says (James 5:12).

- Integrity backs up what it says with how it lives (Titus 2:7).

- Integrity is what God looks for in a person's character (1 Chronicles 29:17).

So, how do you develop integrity? It happens one choice at a time. Your initial decision not to cross a certain line will plant the seed. "I will not cheat" is a decision that places the acorn of integrity in the soil of your heart. But it doesn't stop there. You've got to water it, nurture it, help it to grow. Every time you keep a promise, even though it may come at a high cost, your integrity is watered. Every time you choose to tell the truth when tempted to lie, you strengthen your integrity.

share Him

▶ Strive to consistently walk your talk; be a promise keeper—the trustworthy guy or girl whom others can count on. Integrity is about reputation. It's not a hidden characteristic; it's a public thing.

▶ Understand that integrity is also fragile. One act of deception can ruin trust and scar your witness. Integrity is not so much about getting it; it's about keeping what you already have.

interactive journal

▶ **1 Kings 9:4–5:** Does this passage motivate you to nurture and grow integrity in your life? Why or why not?

_____

_____

_____

Considering that your whole life is on display before God 24/7, list some aspects of your character that you'd like to improve.

my prayer:

answered prayer:

someone to pray for:

communicate

day **5**
be real

"When you witness, don't treat an unbeliever like a project. Give others dignity and respect. See unbelievers with Christ's compassionate eyes. Above all, check your motives. Ask yourself why you witness at all. Is it to meet a church quota and to look spiritual—or is it out of real love and authentic faith?"

"So when you give to the needy, do not announce it with trumpets, as the hypocrites do in the synagogues and on the streets, to be honored by men. I tell you the truth, they have received their reward in full. But when you give to the needy, do not let your left hand know what your right hand is doing, so that your giving may be in secret. Then your Father, who sees what is done in secret, will reward you."

MATTHEW 6:2–4

experience Him

What's your motive when you witness? For that matter, why do you serve Christ and attend church? Is it all just a cultural thing—or is it truly a God thing? When you refer to yourself as *a Christian,* is your description more of a title—or does it describe a real, growing, on-fire faith?

God knows the motives of your heart. He sees everything you do in secret, both good and bad. Jesus once explained to His disciples that the good we do in secret will eventually be rewarded in public. In other words, if you serve God faithfully in secret, God won't keep it secret for long. If you do things just so other people will notice, God will not reward you. But if you do good works just because they are good and because you want to obey God, He will reward you publicly.

share Him

Check out how eighteen-year-old Sean, of Des Moines, Iowa, describes authentic faith: "A real Christian is someone who puts others before himself; someone who doesn't praise God one moment, then gossip about his friends. A true Christian respects others by what he says and through his actions. If we are true imitators of Christ, people will see His love, joy, compassion, and mercy through us. We can witness through our lifestyles. Actions do speak louder than words."

The world needs authentic Christians. You may be the only hope some people have to hear about eternal life. Consider Sean's words, then apply them to your life. Be an imitator of Christ. Be real.

interactive journal

▶ **2 Timothy 4:1–8:** What does it mean to be "poured out like a drink offering"? Does this give a hint to the kind of motivation we must have as Christians?

_____

_____

_____

_____

_____

_____

▶ **1 Peter 2:9–10:** What does it mean to be "a royal priesthood"? How does this effect your walk with Christ?

_____

_____

_____

_____

_____

_____

_____

▶ **Ezekiel 3:16–21:** Does this passage suggest that believers will be held accountable for not sharing their faith? Why or why not?

_____

_____

_____

_____

_____

_____

_____

_____

_____

_____

my prayer:

_____

_____

_____

_____

_____

answered prayer:

_____

_____

_____

_____

someone to pray for:

_____

_____

_____

_____

day **6**

be wise

communicate

"While I attempt to do what's right and to obey God, I often get caught up in unwise choices. Before I know it, I'm heading down the wrong path. What can I do to change?"

> *Be very careful, then, how you live—not as unwise but as wise, making the most of every opportunity, because the days are evil.*
>
> EPHESIANS 5:15–16

experience Him

Discernment. Making wise choices. Living a bold faith in a dark world. Even Christians with the best intentions can get off course from time to time. In his book *Experiencing God,* Henry Blackaby offers some valuable advice that can keep you on the right track: "Through the ages the wisdom found in God's Word has been tested and proven true. It is critical that you measure everything you hear against the Scriptures."[11]

But for those times when you've already made some dumb choices and are unsure about what to do, C. S. Lewis offers some encouragement:

"A live body is not one that never gets hurt, but one that can to some extent repair itself. In the same way a Christian is not a man who never goes wrong, but a man who is enabled to repent and pick himself up and begin over again after each stumble— because the Christ-life is inside him, repairing him all the time, enabling him to repeat (in some degree) the kind of voluntary death that Christ Himself carried out." [12]

Making wise choices involves more than head knowledge. True wisdom is the ability to apply God's truth to everyday situations. And the wisest action a Christian can take is to admit a wrong he or she has committed, turn to Christ (confession), then start fresh again—in the right direction (repentance).

Does God speak wisdom to you through the voices of other Christians? Absolutely. But the advice of others must always be checked against God's Word. Talking with someone in authority and having him pray as you seek to make decisions are wise steps to take. A godly friend can help you stay accountable to your commitments to God—and he or she can help you stay on the right track.

share Him

▶ Disconnect from the world's lies. Be a solid witness by being the kind of Christian who always seeks to stand firmly in

God's truth. "There is a way that seems right to a man, but in the end it leads to death" (Proverbs 14:12).

▶ Evaluate your weak points, then take action. "Let us throw off everything that hinders. . .and let us run with perseverance the race marked out for us" (Hebrews 12:1).

▶ The fact is, you—and only you—are responsible for your actions. Making the right choices, and dealing with the wrong ones, is something you'll have to shoulder all by yourself. So, will you choose to bend the rules from time to time (knowing that you can), or will you commit to an unshakable faith in Christ? *Now* is the time to decide. Like it or not, the days ahead will be filled with all kinds of temptations.

interactive journal

▶ **1 Kings 3:16–28:** Describe Solomon's wisdom in action.

_____

_____

_____

_____

_____

▶ **Proverbs 14:11–14:** How can you keep your life on the right path?

my prayer:

_____
_____
_____
_____
_____

answered prayer:

_____
_____
_____
_____

someone to pray for:

_____
_____
_____
_____

day 7
be consumed by God

communicate

"I have a friend who is absolutely consumed by God. She doesn't have to preach a sermon with words; her lifestyle does it for her. I want that, too. What's her secret? What does it take to be a radically committed Christian?"

"If anyone would come after me, he must deny himself and take up his cross daily and follow me. For whoever wants to save his life will lose it, but whoever loses his life for me will save it."

LUKE 9:23–24

experience Him

What kind of cross do you carry daily? Exactly who or what is the passion of your life? Is getting your career off the ground the most important thing to you? A relationship, maybe? Or could it be money or popularity?

Jesus wants to be your passion; He wants to consume your life. He wants you to carry the cross of Christ. But it involves a choice that only you can make.

FACT:

Your birth and arrival on planet earth was God's idea, not yours. Likewise, your childhood came without thinking. (It required no act of the will.) But committing your life to Christ was a completely different matter. It involved a choice—followed by action: confession, repentance, submission, forgiveness, trust. . .transformation.

FACT:

Radical obedience is also a choice. You have to want it and go after it with all your heart. You've got to exercise your will. If you don't choose the deeper things of God, you'll remain a "spiritual child," regardless of how grown-up and wise you think you are. The sad truth is too many Christians spend their lives crawling around in "spiritual diapers."

FACT:

Jesus doesn't ask us to add a little of Himself into our daily walk—He asks to *become* our lives. He's not interested in people who dabble in a relationship with Him, He's interested in people who *live* Him—faithfully, consistently, day by day.

Revelation 3:15–16 says, "I know your deeds, that you are neither cold nor hot. I wish you were either one or the other!

So, because you are lukewarm—neither hot nor cold—I am about to spit you out of my mouth."

The point is this: Jesus is not interested in people who play church. He's interested in people who are the church—people who are a living, breathing, loving part of His body—people who are totally committed to Him. What's more, God loves us too much to "leave us in diapers." He wants us to grow up—mentally, physically, spiritually, and socially—just like His Son (Luke 2:52).

share Him

- Do some soul-searching. Do you truly want to make knowing, serving, loving, and communicating God your number one passion? Or are you more like the multitudes described in the New Testament—people who were just hanging around Jesus for another free meal, or because that's where their friends were, or because they wanted to use Jesus for selfish motives?

- Strive to make Christ your first thought in the morning, your constant companion throughout the day, the Man you imitate in public, and your last thought at night. Consider what He wants for your life, and place it above your personal desires.

interactive journal

▶ **Colossians 1:28–29:** We are to tell others about Jesus. Yet how can we effectively do this if we lack true passion for Him? How can you deepen your walk with Jesus?

_____

_____

_____

_____

_____

▶ **Hebrews 12:5–6:** Why does the Lord discipline those He loves? How can it steer you clear of danger and help your faith to grow?

_____

_____

_____

_____

_____

▶ **Matthew 22:37–40:** Memorize and seek to live out this passage. Jot down some faith goals.

_____

_____

my prayer:

answered prayer:

someone to pray for:

interacting with Christ

break the sin barriers

day 8
unconfessed sin

communicate

"I feel as if there's a giant invisible wall between God and me. Maybe it's my guilty conscience. I have sinned in a number of ways lately—but I just don't know how to talk to Him about it."

> But because of your stubbornness and your unrepentant heart, you are storing up wrath against yourself for the day of God's wrath, when his righteous judgment will be revealed. God "will give to each person according to what he has done." To those who by persistence in doing good seek glory, honor and immortality, he will give eternal life. But for those who are self-seeking and who reject the truth and follow evil, there will be wrath and anger.
>
> ROMANS 2:5–8

experience Him

There's an old saying that goes something like this: "Sin will take you further than you want to go, cost you more than you want to pay, and keep you longer than you want to stay."

Simply put, sin is disobedience to God's will and the implementation of our own plan. When we rebel against God, it's as if our actions say that He doesn't know what He's talking about, His Word is outdated, and He isn't trustworthy. But when we say *yes* to God and trust His will—even in small ways—we bring Him glory. Our actions say that His commands are good and that He deserves to be obeyed.

Bottom line: If we want God's blessing on our lives, if we want to know Him intimately and be an effective witness for Him, submission to His will and His Word is nonnegotiable. (Check out Deuteronomy 4:2.)

share Him

▶ There doesn't have to be a "giant invisible wall" that separates you from God. You don't have to live with a huge load of guilt and shame in your life. Christ is reaching out to you with open arms—go to Him in prayer. Tell Him all about your sins, tell Him you're sorry, and He'll forgive you. In Jesus, you'll find acceptance, love, and freedom—despite your shortcomings.

Understand that following Christ is not a passing fad. It's a step-by-step, day-by-day commitment. And like any relationship, it requires your time and devotion in order for it to grow. "Test everything. Hold on to the good. Avoid every kind of evil" (1 Thessalonians 5:21–22).

interactive journal

▶ **Genesis 19:1–29:** Why does unchecked sin always result in destruction?

_____

_____

_____

_____

_____

_____

_____

_____

_____

_____

▶ **1 Timothy 1:12–20:** How has Christ shown mercy to you?

my prayer:

answered prayer:

_____
_____
_____
_____
_____
_____
_____

someone to pray for:

_____
_____
_____
_____
_____
_____

day **9**

take off your mask

communicate

"I'm afraid to let people see the real me, because I know they won't like the person inside. I guess that's why witnessing is so hard for me. I'd rather keep relationships at a distance."

For we are God's workmanship, created in Christ Jesus to do good works, which God prepared in advance for us to do.

EPHESIANS 2:10

experience Him

Have you ever gone to a costume party? If you have, then you know how creative people can be, concocting elaborate outfits that can completely disguise a person's identity. On occasion, you can figure out who's behind the mask, especially if you know the person well—his mannerisms, his cologne, his voice.

Masks do a good job of hiding things, don't they? Not just at a party, but throughout the year. If we're honest, we'll admit that we have many of them at our disposal. We use makeup to hide a blemish. We wear trendy clothes or drive a new car to impress others. We force a smile to conceal the misery we feel inside. We may even point a finger at someone else in order to avoid facing our own shortcomings.

When it comes to our relationship with God, we simply cannot hide behind masks. While people focus on the outward appearance, God sees our hearts. He knows our deepest secrets. He understands our true motives. "Do not be deceived: God cannot be mocked" (Galatians 6:7). We can fool others. We can even fool ourselves. But we can never fool God.

share Him

▸ Understand what God really thinks of you. We've all heard that He loves us. And we know that God allowed His Son, Jesus Christ, to die on a cross and pay the penalty of our sin—which demonstrates the extent of His love. Then why don't we act as if this is the most incredible news we've ever heard? If God created us in His image (Genesis 1:27) to do good works that He prepared in advance for us to do (Ephesians 2:10), why do we hide behind masks? And why do we pursue what our culture thinks is cool in order to feel good about ourselves?

When we stand before God on Judgment Day, all the secrets we've spent our lives hiding from other people will be made public. God will accept no excuses. Does this sound harsh? Does it frighten you? Then pull off your mask and confess your sins. Ask Jesus to forgive you. Ask Him to help you face your shortcomings and to do a deep healing in your life. He will answer this prayer.

interactive journal

Exodus 20:22–26: What do these verses tell you about the value of human life?

_____

_____

_____

_____

_____

_____

_____

_____

Psalm 139:1–4: How does being known so intimately by God make you feel about yourself?

_____

_____

_____

_____

_____

_____

_____

my prayer:

_____

_____

_____

_____

_____

answered prayer:

someone to pray for:

day **10**

don't be a
people pleaser

communicate

"Brains, beauty, bucks—these are the things the world values. Yet, even as a Christian, I find myself getting caught up in this same shallow mind-set. How can I rise above this? How can I set my priorities straight?"

"Enter through the narrow gate. For wide is the gate and broad is the road that leads to destruction, and many enter through it. But small is the gate and narrow the road that leads to life, and only a few find it."

MATTHEW 7:13–14

experience Him

It's a sad fact of human nature—even for Christians. If we're not playing "the performance game" at school or at work or among our circle of friends, we end up committing social suicide. Playing "the game" means doing what's socially acceptable: getting into the right school, making the team, landing that prestigious job, dating and marrying the pretty people, wearing the right clothes, living in the biggest house on the block, going to the right parties, making your first million by age thirty.

For many in our culture, social survival is dependent on how we measure up in these areas, right? And if we don't measure up, we're not successful. . .and if we're not successful, we're not part of the "in" crowd. So we spend every waking moment playing the performance game, trying to prove our worth. But what happens if we can't compete? We end up feeling pretty bad about ourselves. We begin thinking that we're inferior—convinced that we just don't measure up in life.

Of course, there are exceptions to this shallow game. There are people who aren't caught up in what others think—people who don't attempt to prove their worth through impressive titles or the latest toys.

Take, for example, the guys and girls on campus who spend spring break serving at a South American orphanage. Or that lady at the office who visits shut-ins three times a week. Or that kid on the football team who isn't afraid to pray before a game.

share Him

▶ Vow to be different. The key is allowing the Holy Spirit and the truth of the Bible to saturate your heart, mind, and soul. Let the One who created you and everything in this world navigate your life—not the so-called popular people. Let the

God of all eternity define your worth—not the acquisition of material things.

▶ While most Christians understand that their lives could—and *should*—be a reflection of Jesus Christ, they allow peer fear to get in the way. Jesus said, "Then you will know the truth, and the truth will set you free" (John 8:32). Are you among the many who haven't allowed the truth to set them free? If so, it's time for a change.

interactive journal

▶ **Ephesians 5:8–10:** List some things that you can do to please the Lord.

Romans 8:18–25: Why do you think a life committed to God is far more fulfilling than a worldly existence?

_____

_____

_____

_____

_____

_____

my prayer:

_____

_____

_____

_____

_____

_____

_____

answered prayer:

_____

_____

_____

_____

_____

someone to pray for:

_____

_____

_____

_____

_____

day **II**

punched out by pride?

communicate

"I have to admit that, even after committing my life to Christ, my pride often reared its ugly head. Too often, my life was governed by ambition and the desire to get rather than to give. My advice: Put to death your pride, and come to life in Christ."

Do nothing out of selfish ambition or vain conceit, but in humility consider others better than yourselves. Each of you should look not only to your own interests, but also to the interests of others.

PHILIPPIANS 2:3–4

experience Him

Pride. Here's a definition worth reviewing: (a) an overhigh opinion of oneself; exaggerated self-esteem; conceit; (b) haughty behavior resulting from this; arrogance.

Though pride practically rules our culture, it's certainly

nothing new. Pride is a sin that was just as destructive in biblical days as it is today. Scripture is filled with warnings about pride:

- In 2 Chronicles 26:3–5, when King Uzziah was first crowned at age sixteen, he "sought God." But as he became older and more powerful, he became more and more prideful. When he tried to burn incense in the temple—a privilege reserved for priests—he was struck with leprosy (see 2 Chronicles 26:16–21).

- The Lord warned of judgment for the vain in Isaiah 3:16–17: "The women of Zion are haughty, walking along with outstretched necks, flirting with their eyes. . . . Therefore the Lord will bring sores on the heads of the women of Zion; the Lord will make their scalps bald."

- Christ shocked the Pharisees He was dining with by saying, "For everyone who exalts himself will be humbled, and he who humbles himself will be exalted" (Luke 14:11).

- Solomon, who tasted incredible success, wealth, and ultimately emptiness, conceded, "When pride comes, then comes disgrace, but with humility comes wisdom" (Proverbs 11:2).

- He also discovered this shocker: "Like a gold ring in a pig's snout is a woman who shows no discretion" (Proverbs 11:22).

share Him

- Keep in mind that Christians can be knocked out by pride. We are often tempted to forget who made us and whose we are. We live in tension. Pride and selfishness struggle desperately to elbow humility and tenderness right out of our lives.

▶ Seek to rid yourself of self-promoting, self-seeking, self-satisfying, and just plain selfish attitudes. As Christians, our role model is God's Son. He didn't wear flashy clothing, give autographs, or even demand to be called "Prince" (though He certainly is). He was a servant of mankind, filled with love and humility. He taught forgiveness, servitude, and trust in God for everything—yet He is the most famous man to ever live.

interactive journal

▶ **Philippians 2:1–11:** What specific steps can you take to overcome pride and selfishness, and to become more like Christ?

_____

_____

_____

_____

_____

Luke 23:32–49: Jot down your thoughts on how Christ's actions described here represent the ultimate act of selflessness.

_____

_____

_____

_____

_____

_____

_____

_____

my prayer:

_____

_____

_____

_____

_____

_____

answered prayer:

_____

_____

_____

_____

_____

someone to pray for:

_____

_____

_____

_____

_____

interacting with Christ

day **12**
forgive and forget

"I'm really a messed up person—and have a hard time believing that Jesus truly forgives me for the things I've done. In fact, I'll never be able to forgive myself."

For as high as the heavens are above the earth, so great is his love for those who fear him; as far as the east is from the west, so far has he removed our transgressions from us.

PSALM 103:11–12

experience Him

Never?! You'll *never* be able to forgive yourself? You'll be forever stuck in your wrongs?

Even though it's hard to accept or to understand, if you've gotten on your knees and have asked the Lord to forgive you, your sins have been pardoned. God has even forgotten them. "I will forgive their wickedness and will remember their sins no more" (Jeremiah 31:34).

Of course, it's hard to believe because we are human, and God is God. His thoughts are not our thoughts. His ways are not our ways. He loves us so much, He pardons our sinful souls and gives us a fresh start. He hits the delete key on the computer, and the screen is blank.

He simply doesn't remember that awful lie you told or that item you stole or that kiss that almost went too far. . .the sins you remember only too well—those terrible things that are still haunting you, making your life miserable.

To the Lord, yesterday's sins—the ones that you have already confessed to Him—are forgiven and forgotten. As hard as it may be, try to get your mind off "yesterday." Live in the hope and promise of today.

share Him

▶ Christ offers you freedom from your sins—accept it! And communicate this Good News to others. Understand that whenever you foul up, whenever you make a mistake, Jesus is there to forgive you. He's always there to pick you up and to help you get back on your feet.

▶ Remember how Christ operates. He doesn't clobber us over the head with guilt. He doesn't go around sulking, holding it over our heads, or trying to make us feel low. He just gently and tenderly tells us that we are forgiven. That's it, end of discussion.

interactive journal

▶ **Hebrews 8:7–13:** Consider ways you can share this Good
News with those around you.

_____

_____

_____

_____

_____

_____

_____

_____

_____

_____

_____

▶ Make a list of people in your life you need to forgive.

_____

_____

_____

my prayer:

answered prayer:

someone to pray for:

communicate

day 13
neglected prayer

"How can I break through God's silence? I'm a Christian, but I don't sense His presence in my life. In fact, my faith is really losing some of its fire. I want to change. I want unbelievers to see Jesus through my lifestyle."

The eyes of the Lord are on the righteous and his ears are attentive to their cry.

PSALM 34:15

experience Him

Whenever people say their spiritual life has lost its spark, one question comes to mind: How's your prayer life?

While Bible reading, study groups, and worship services are important ways of growing your faith, the primary way God draws us closer to Him is through prayer. Prayer is intimate. Prayer is interactive.

Adam and Eve had daily walks and conversations with their Maker. Noah spoke constantly to the Almighty. Abraham had an intense, powerful prayer relationship with the heavenly Father. So did Isaac, Jacob, and Joseph. The Israelites in captivity had nothing but prayer to connect them to the Living God. It wasn't until after they were brought out of captivity and on their way to the Promised Land that the first of God's words were ever written down.

Praying was the first means of connection with God, and it's every bit as powerful today as it was in biblical times. Prayer is the lifeblood of our walk with God. If you aren't praying, you're killing yourself.

share Him

Ask yourself some questions:

True/False.
My interest in faith is equal to other interests in my life: relationships with the opposite sex, sports, music. . .

True/False.
Bible reading bores me to death.

True/False.
Sometimes I go weeks without praying.

True/False.
God often seems distant to me.

If you answered *true* to even one of the questions, you need to ask yourself a few questions: Is God the most important person in my life. . .or am I allowing other pursuits to push Him out of my life? Are spiritual things really boring. . .or are things of this world my priority? Do I truly expect God to speak to me through prayer. . .or am I just going through the motions?

▶ Move beyond "baby spirituality" and seek the deeper things of Christ: "When I was a child, I talked like a child, I thought like a child, I reasoned like a child. When I became a man, I put childish ways behind me" (1 Corinthians 13:11).

▶ Stop making excuses—and pray! Jesus is your best friend. Just as you talk to other friends in your life, He wants you to tell Him about everything going on in your life: your praises, the desires of your heart and your struggles.

interactive journal

▶ **Proverbs 15:29:** Based on this verse, what do think could end up hindering your prayers?

_____

_____

_____

_____

_____

_____

_____

Matthew 26:36–39: Why do you think Jesus stresses the importance of being alone to pray?

_____

_____

_____

_____

_____

_____

_____

_____

my prayer:

answered prayer:

someone to pray for:

day **14**

no Lone Ranger Christians

communicate

"When Sunday morning rolls around, I never feel like going to church. Why is it so important to worship God in a sanctuary? Why can't I do it on my own?"

It was he who gave some to be apostles, some to be prophets, some to be evangelists, and some to be pastors and teachers, to prepare God's people for works of service, so that the body of Christ may be built up until we all reach unity in the faith and in the knowledge of the Son of God and become mature, attaining to the whole measure of the fullness of Christ.

EPHESIANS 4:11–13

experience Him

Let's be honest. We all wake up from time to time on Sunday with the strong temptation to worship at

"Bedside Baptist" or "First Church of the Water Bed." But if we're wise, we fight off the temptation.

Here are two key reasons why church attendance is important:

I.

There's no such thing as the Lone Ranger Christian. Worshiping God is meant to be shared with others. Even if you can't understand everything the pastor says—or if you can't find the book of Malachi if your life depended upon it—spending time in church teaches you that God's family is a whole lot bigger than your own. And get this: Heaven is going be packed with all kinds of people praising and worshiping God. Church is a good place to prepare. What's more, our church family keeps us accountable.

2.

Going to church plugs you in to God's truth. Face it, we encounter a lot of distractions during the week—at school or work, on TV, in our relationships. Too many things can pull us away from God. Sunday mornings give us a spiritual *ZAP*—and get us back on track.

share Him

▶ Fight the temptation to sleep in on Sunday mornings. Make church attendance a priority. God wants to shape the mature Christian inside of you. That's His will. The God of the universe has determined for you to "become mature, attaining to the whole measure of the fullness of Christ" (Ephesians 4:13).

Get involved and serve at your church. God wants you to see it as an honor, not a drag. Why? Because He's calling you to deal with His people, the flock whom He loves. It's your chance to serve Him by serving others.

interactive journal

1 Peter 5:1–7: Why is the list of responsibilities mentioned not exclusive to church officers? How does this list apply to you?

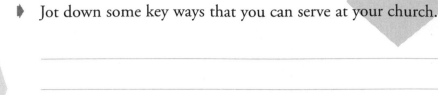

♦ Jot down some key ways that you can serve at your church.

my prayer:

answered prayer:

_____

_____

_____

_____

_____

someone to pray for:

_____

_____

_____

_____

know and do God's will

day 15

God's will:
the "DUH" factor

communicate

"As a Christian, how can I clue in to God's will for my life? And exactly how do I tune in to His voice every day?"

For you know what instructions we gave you by the authority of the Lord Jesus. It is God's will that you should be sanctified.

1 THESSALONIANS 4:2–3

experience Him

Getting a clue about God's will involves a simple step that will point you in the right direction: understanding The DUH Factor. In the verse above (1 Thessalonians 4:3), what does the apostle Paul mean when he says that we should be sanctified? It sounds like something that happens to coffee beans, right? (But for your information, that word is *Sanka-fied*—a totally different concept!)

Sanctification is when something is set apart for a special purpose. Spiritually speaking, it's when we set aside our gifts, bodies, and plans for God's purposes. It means we live a disciplined life so God can use us in a special way. Okay, we know what you're thinking: *That's great, but I just want to know whether I should eat Cocoa Puffs or Cap'n Crunch!*

That's where The DUH Factor comes in.

Your life is filled with lots of simple situations that are easy to figure out—situations that belong in the "DUH" category. (Choosing to tell the truth, never cheating or stealing.) These kinds of circumstances require a basic knowledge of understanding *right* from *wrong*. And, of course, the place we turn for truth—absolute truth—is the Holy Bible.

share Him

Get a clue about God's will for your life by tuning in to His Word. The Bible is timeless and absolutely, positively accurate in everything He knew was essential for us to know. That's far more trustworthy than our feelings, which change hour by hour. While there is room for debate on secondary issues (such as when the Rapture will occur), there are no discrepancies in God's promises, commands, and warnings. And the fact is, archaeologists and researchers are constantly making new discoveries that confirm the Bible's authority.

interactive journal

▶ **Romans 12:1–8:** How should you "test and approve what God's will is"?

_____

_____

_____

_____

_____

_____

_____

_____

_____

_____

_____

▶ **Genesis 12:2:** Based on this verse, what's God's will for your life?

_____

_____

_____

my prayer:

answered prayer:

someone to pray for:

interacting with Christ

day 16

the "R" factor

communicate

"What should I do when I'm struggling with a really tough decision and I need God's specific direction? How do I figure out His will in these kinds of situations?"

> *Therefore, I urge you, brothers, in view of God's mercy, to offer your bodies as living sacrifices, holy and pleasing to God—this is your spiritual act of worship. Do not conform any longer to the pattern of this world, but be transformed by the renewing of your mind. Then you will be able to test and approve what God's will is—his good, pleasing and perfect will.*
>
> ROMANS 12:1–2

experience Him

Exactly how do you know for sure if God wants you to go on that missions trip next summer or give up a certain friendship? How do you get a clue about what God wants you to do with your life? This is where the all-important "R" factor comes into play. What does the *R* stand for? *Rough? Radical? Run?* Nope. It represents *RELATIONSHIP!*

When you have a close relationship with Jesus, He will tell you Himself what He wants you to do. He communicates with you throughout the day, answering your questions and guiding your steps. You literally walk in His presence minute by minute.

Does God talk to people with an audible voice? Let's clear up this misconception once and for all. The answer: Not usually. In fact, He rarely communicates with most of us this way, if ever. Instead, the Holy Spirit deals with each human being in a personal and intimate way, convicting, directing, and influencing us. God has promised to speak to our hearts, so we can expect Him to, but He is not compelled to tell us everything we want to know the moment we desire the information. Therefore, it's important that we nurture a consistent, growing relationship with Him.

share Him

▶ Keep in mind that when you have an intimate relationship with Jesus, not only will He help you through difficult situations when they come up; oftentimes, He will prepare you for them in advance.

▶ Tune in to the spiritual discernment the Holy Spirit provides. This awareness takes on a "something's not quite right" feeling when God is trying to get you to avoid a course of action—or when danger is lurking nearby. On the other hand, peace and a sense of confidence are the signs of spiritual awareness that God gives when you're on the right track. And as you grow closer and closer to Him, your instincts will become more sensitive to His influence. Your entire mind and spirit will become more in tune to God, and you'll begin to hear Him more clearly, just as with any good friend.

▶ Understand that we learn God's will for our lives minute by minute and practice after practice. As we love Him and live in Him, His voice becomes clearer and clearer—and His Word in us grows stronger. That is His will for you forever. . . the rest is just details. Right? DUH!

interactive journal

▶ **Isaiah 30:19–22:** Whose voice must we listen to?

_____

_____

_____

_____

▸ **Romans 8:28–39:** How can you be confident that God is for you—even when things aren't going your way?

my prayer:

answered prayer:

someone to pray for:

day 17

career and calling

"I'm interested in a number of different careers, but I'm clueless about which path to follow. My parents want me to go for something marketable. My pastor thinks I should be a missionary. My friends say something creative is more my thing. How should I find my fit?"

The Lord is near to all who call on him, to all who call on him in truth. He fulfills the desires of those who fear him; he hears their cry and saves them.

PSALM 145:18–19

communicate

experience Him

When it comes to discovering our career and calling, what makes some people successful, while others seem to flounder? Let's cut right to the chase with an answer: You'll find your unique place in this world—and, ultimately, true fulfillment—if you *fit yourself into what God wants for you rather than what you want for yourself.*

God created each of us with the abilities and talents to serve Him in very specific and significant ways. Successful Christians know this—and they've found their place within the body. They don't waste their God-given talent on pursuits that counter God's will. They are guided by a clear personal vision of what Christ wants them to accomplish in life—an accurate and precise picture of the work that expresses them best. They have identified their talents and are using them. As a result, these individuals experience profound and lasting benefits: reduced stress, more balance, a more productive career, and a more satisfying life.

share Him

▶ Pick a profession that's in tune with God's will for your life by taking your dreams and desires to God and trusting Him with the outcome. Is the Lord directing your steps? If so, Proverbs 16:3 promises that you're on the right track: "Commit to the Lord whatever you do, and your plans will succeed." But keep in mind that your plans have no strength if they're not from God.

▶ Consult with wise Christian people and seriously consider their counsel as you plot your course. Let trusted people know about your dreams and aspirations. Their input can be most valuable in finding the life pursuit that will best shape the person inside you.

▶ Consider the gifts and talents God has given you. Ask God

to reveal what His "good, pleasing and perfect will" looks like for you (Romans 12:2).

▶ Pursue what is kind, just, and loving even if you don't make as much money: "Better a little with righteousness than much gain with injustice" (Proverbs 16:8).

interactive journal

▶ **Colossians 2:6–8:** Why is it important to be "rooted and built up" in God—especially when it comes to your life's calling?

2 Peter 1:1–11: List how God's divine power has kept you on the right path.

_____

_____

_____

_____

_____

_____

_____

_____

2 Kings 18:1–8: What is God's definition of success?

_____

_____

_____

_____

_____

_____

_____

my prayer:

_____
_____
_____
_____
_____
_____

answered prayer:

_____
_____
_____
_____
_____

someone to pray for:

_____
_____
_____
_____
_____

day **18**

setting goals

communicate

"There's so much I want to do in life—I just don't know what steps to take to accomplish my dreams. What's next for me? Continue my education? Find a job? Start a business? Where do I begin?"

In his heart a man plans his course, but the Lord determines his steps.

PROVERBS 16:9

experience Him

Goals for life have similarities to goals in sports. You strive to attain them. There's joy in achieving them. You long to execute them again.

As you set goals for yourself, realize that the Lord may have other plans for you. Remember the apostle Paul? He initially wanted to spend his life wiping out Christianity. God, however, from Paul's birth had planned for him to be His greatest missionary. (Remember, the Lord is the One who will determine your steps.)

There are three things you've got to remember about a life goal: It's specific, measurable, and attainable.

A specific goal is one you can put into words.

A vague desire to "be a strong Christian" is not very specific. But "join Intervarsity Christian Fellowship my freshman year" is a solid goal.

A measurable goal is one that allows you to see progress.

"Know the Bible from cover to cover" is tough to measure. But "read the New Testament this summer" allows you to mark your progress with that little bookmark in your Bible.

An attainable goal is one that can reasonably be completed.

"Lead the world to Christ" is both concrete and measurable, but hardly attainable. "Introduce three people to Jesus before I graduate from college" is a goal that meets all three criteria.

share Him

▶ Determine to set your goals and dreams in motion. Take an afternoon, a weekend, or an hour a day for a month—whatever you need—and pray. Above all, listen to God. Focus on His voice and direction for your life.

▶ Next, begin writing some specific, measurable, attainable goals for your life. Setting life goals shouldn't be a one-time affair.

interactive journal

▶ **Galatians 1:13–16:** Describe how Paul was set apart from birth and called by God's grace.

_____

_____

_____

_____

_____

_____

_____

_____

_____

_____

▶ **Proverbs 16:1–9:** After reading this passage, are you confident that the Lord is the Author of your dreams? What specific things can you do to fit your goals into His plans?

_____

_____

_____

my prayer:

answered prayer:

_____

_____

_____

_____

_____

someone to pray for:

_____

_____

_____

_____

know and do God's will

day **19**

marriage or singleness?

communicate

"I've been in a lot of relationships, but I haven't yet met the right person, and I just don't have a sense if marriage is in my future. What steps can I take to ensure that I choose wisely?"

"I know the plans I have for you," declares the Lord, "plans to prosper you and not to harm you, plans to give you hope and a future."

JEREMIAH 29:11

experience Him

Marriage or singleness? It's an important question—yet it's probably one that you don't have to think seriously about until many years down the road. Regardless, there are crucial "faith steps" you can take now to help you build a future that is pleasing to the Lord—whether you end up married or remain single.

share Him

FAITH STEP 1:

Next to committing your life to Jesus Christ, choosing a life mate is one of the biggest decisions you'll ever make. Therefore, enter romantic relationships carefully, soberly, and with your eyes wide open. A good marriage is a blessing from the Lord.

FAITH STEP 2:

God doesn't expect you to search the earth for the *one-and-only* person He has in mind for you. (What are the chances of ever finding that person?)

FAITH STEP 3:

Make Jesus, and His will for your life, the center of your desires. He should define your self-worth. Not the status of being in a relationship.

FAITH STEP 4:

Pursue purity. Nothing can ruin a relationship quicker than going too far, too fast, too soon.

FAITH STEP 5:

Understand that singleness is actually a gift that God gives to some people. "I wish that all men were as I am. But each man has his own gift from God; one has this gift, another has that" (1 Corinthians 7:7). In this passage, Paul tells how he was determined to use this special gift as a way to serve and encourage other Christians. Because he did not have a wife, he knew he could devote himself wholeheartedly to his ministry.

interactive journal

▶ **1 Corinthians 13:4–8:** Tell why the kind of love described here is the kind that should be shared with a marriage partner.

▶ If marriage is a future goal for you, describe the kind of person you want as a life mate.

_____

_____

_____

_____

_____

_____

▶ If you're convinced that God is calling you to singleness, tell why you think He is giving you this gift.

_____

_____

_____

_____

_____

_____

_____

my prayer:

answered prayer:

someone to pray for:

day**20**
handling hardships

communicate

"My life is being slammed by so many problems right now. I wake up every morning wondering, *What else can possibly go wrong?* I know that being a Christian doesn't mean life is going to be smooth all the time, but I feel so overwhelmed. How can I cope?"

> *We are hard pressed on every side, but not crushed; perplexed, but not in despair; persecuted, but not abandoned; struck down, but not destroyed.*
>
> 2 CORINTHIANS 4:8–9

experience Him

Some mornings we wake up and can't help feeling as though our life is in the path of a speeding freight train. A friend blabs some of your deepest secrets. The person you've been dating suddenly decides the two of you "are annoyingly incompatible." Your grandfather dies of heart failure. You just can't figure out where you fit in.

The circumstances seem hopeless, and we feel frightened and alone. Doubts scream in our minds. *Get up—and run! Or be flattened beyond recognition!*

But the Bible tells you something different: "Stay put! Pray. And trust God." Good advice. In fact, Psalm 91:1 says, "He who dwells in the shelter of the Most High will rest in the shadow of the Almighty."

Whether your circumstances blast in quicker than you can recover or your door is constantly open when sin knocks, God can set you free if you allow Him. He won't always take away the problems or temptations, but He *will* faithfully enter the difficulty with you and provide a way out.

What's more, He always causes everything to turn out for your benefit. No matter how hopeless the outlook, *don't run!* God will help you through it!

share Him

▶ When times get tough and doubt creeps in, the Bible is the book you should crack open. Not only will you learn how others dealt with doubt, but also how God dealt with His people when they doubted. Check out John the Baptist's trials in Matthew 11:1–19. Or check out the doubt dilemma of Thomas—aka doubting Thomas—in John 14:1–7.

▶ Keep in mind that God fully understands that His people battle through periods of doubt and fear—especially during tough trials. His Son went through difficult times. Think about Gethsemane. Jesus prayed, anguished, and sweat blood. But He followed the Father's plan. Jesus didn't come to condemn. He knows that we live in a fallen world. He came as a man and lived on earth—to save us. He has compassion for His people. It's not what you did or couldn't do that counts, it's what He did for you. All He asks is that you let Him into your heart. He stands, knocks, and patiently waits with open arms and listening ears. Won't you let Him in?

interactive journal

▶ **John 14:15–27:** How will Jesus comfort us in times of trouble?

_____

_____

_____

_____

_____

_____

_____

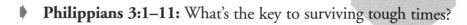

▶ **Philippians 3:1–11:** What's the key to surviving tough times?

_____

_____

_____

_____

_____

_____

_____

_____

_____

my prayer:

_____

_____

_____

_____

_____

answered prayer:

_____

_____

_____

_____

_____

someone to pray for:

_____

_____

_____

_____

know and do God's will

day **21**

the wonder
of worship

"I feel as if I'm in a mud-oozing rut with God. I'm bored with church—and catch myself wondering if Christianity really makes a difference in my life. How can I give my spiritual passion a much-needed zap?"

"Yet a time is coming and has now come when the true worshipers will worship the Father in spirit and truth, for they are the kind of worshipers the Father seeks."

JOHN 4:23

experience Him

Like most Christians, your faith can get pretty dry at times. But the living water Jesus gives can transform the most desolate, desert-like soul into an abundant life spring! The truth is, worshiping God is an interactive experience. "Come near to God and he will come near to you" (James 4:8). It's both private and public. It involves your heart and your head. And as you linger in God's presence, praising Him, it's like you get a high-voltage spiritual zap. Worship builds you into a stronger Christian.

As you worship God, you SHOULD . . .

. . .give Him your praise and glory.

. . .give Him your thanks.

. . .give Him your whole heart.

As you worship God, you SHOULDN'T . . .

. . .go through the motions of an empty ritual.

. . .approach Him with wrong motives, using your praise as a means of getting something.

. . .treat this special time as an option in your life.

Don't treat worship like drudgery or a burden. God is the great and awesome King, and His name is great among the nations. He can and will raise up true worshipers from around the globe. The question is, will you be one of them?

share Him

It's time to get F.A.T. (faithful, available, teachable):

▶ Know that being a FAITHFUL person of God means trusting that He is in your life—even when you don't sense His presence and He seems a million miles away from the worship service.

- Commit to being AVAILABLE to Christ. Make knowing Him the priority in your life 24/7—not just for a couple of hours at church. Be available daily by spending time reading the Bible, praying, and worshiping Him.

- Be TEACHABLE. Before the choir begins to sing—and well before the pastor steps up to the pulpit—pray something like this: "Lord, help me to concentrate today. I want to tune in to Your voice and Your instruction for my life. Draw me close to You and transform me into the kind of person You want me to be. Amen."

interactive journal

- **John 4:1–26:** What kind of worshiper does God seek? (Hint: the kind who worships Him in spirit and truth.) What does Jesus offer? (Here's another hint: living water.)

_____

_____

_____

_____

_____

▶ Personal Psalm: Read a few psalms in the Bible and then
write out your own psalm to God.

_____

_____

_____

_____

_____

_____

_____

_____

_____

_____

_____

my prayer:

answered prayer:

someone to pray for:

take the Isaiah 52 challenge

day **22**
beautiful feet

communicate

"What Christian could possibly keep quiet about forgiveness, salvation, and eternal life with Jesus Christ?! Being a Christian means having a lot to celebrate. I can't keep quiet. I've got to go out into the world with the Good News!"

> *How beautiful on the mountains are the feet of*
> *those who bring Good News, who proclaim peace,*
> *who bring good tidings, who proclaim salvation, who*
> *say to Zion, "Your God reigns!"*
>
> ISAIAH 52:7

experience Him

The Isaiah 52 challenge begins with your feet. That's right! Those stinky, aching feet carry the Good News about history's most amazing feat: "For God so loved the world that he gave his one and only Son, that whoever believes in him shall not perish but have eternal life" (John 3:16).

Our call, if we consider ourselves followers of Jesus Christ, is to move out on beautiful feet (that requires getting off one's beautiful seat!) and take the gospel to the ends of the earth.

The message we're called to carry is nothing short of mind-boggling! Think about it: The holy God who is the *perfect judge* couldn't overlook our sin. But the loving and compassionate God who is our *Father* didn't want us to perish. So, in effect, He first judged our penalty to be death, then stepped down from the judgment seat and sent His only Son, Jesus, to pay that penalty for us.

Now consider this: If Jesus had stayed in the grave after His bloody death, there wouldn't be much hope for humanity. But death couldn't keep Jesus down! He broke out of the tomb, and by His resurrection, declared that death itself would die.

And Jesus didn't just die for us; He rose to live through us, to love through us, and to help us live out God's plan.

share Him

▶ Ask Jesus to give you a heart and passion for evangelism. Ask Him to open your ears and eyes to the lost. Then look for ways to reach out, making the most of every opportunity.

▶ Where should you begin sharing your faith? Look around you. There are people everywhere who probably can't spell Isaiah but who need you to take the Isaiah 52 challenge.

Communicate with them. Share the One who can transform their lives.

interactive journal

▶ **Isaiah 52:7:** Write down all the places those beautiful feet can take you.

_____

_____

_____

_____

_____

_____

_____

_____

_____

_____

_____

▶ Write your testimony. Tell what God's "beautiful feat" (salvation through Jesus Christ) means to you.

_____

_____

_____

_____

_____

_____

_____

_____

▶ **John 13:1–17:** Why did Jesus wash His disciples' feet? What did this beautiful activity communicate to the world?

_____

_____

_____

_____

_____

_____

_____

my prayer:

answered prayer:

someone to pray for:

day 23
show them Jesus

"I encounter so many skeptics who refuse to believe that Jesus is Lord and Savior. How can I open their eyes to the truth?"

"If anyone is thirsty, let him come to me and drink. Whoever believes in me, as the Scripture has said, streams of living water will flow from within him."

JOHN 7:37–38

experience Him

During biblical times, some of the people who encountered Jesus called Him "a good man" and a "prophet"—others claimed He was a trickster. Interestingly, only a fraction of the masses paid any attention to who He really is. (Not too different from today, right?)

In John 7:1–44, Jesus shows up at the Feast of Tabernacles and makes His appearance at the temple court (the very center of the Jewish religion). He begins to teach, and the bigwigs are pretty impressed. They want to know how He got so smart without attending Jerusalem U.

"My teaching is not my own. It comes from him who sent me. If anyone chooses to do God's will, he will find out whether my teaching comes from God or whether I speak on my own. He who speaks on his own does so to gain honor for himself, but he who works for the honor of the one who sent him is a man of truth; there is nothing false about him" (John 7:16–18).

At this, the words really began to fly. Some called Him "demon-possessed," and attempted to seize Him (yet no one was able to lay a hand upon Him). Still, many in the crowd put their faith in Jesus.

share Him

- Jesus wants us to know the truth. He wants us to understand that true satisfaction can't be found in romantic relationships, money, popularity, or beefed-up brain cells. Our most urgent need is the eternal life that only He can give. Yet the world today, just as it was in biblical times, is stubborn, fallen, and blinded to the truth. Jesus won't force anyone to accept the truth. Instead, He just makes Himself available.

- How about you? As a follower of Christ, have you made yourself available to others? Do you have the courage to stand up for Jesus in the face of opposition—or do you find your faith being trampled by your friends? Does your light shine among others—or are you more like a burnt-out lightbulb?

- Make sure that your heart is sincere—that you truly believe that Christ is who He says He is. Do a little soul-searching. . . and ask God to help you work through any doubts that you may have.

- Follow the instruction of Hebrews 12:2: "Let us fix our eyes on Jesus, the author and perfecter of our faith, who for the joy set before him endured the cross, scorning its shame."

interactive journal

- **John 18:37:** How did Jesus describe His reason for being born?

_____

_____

_____

_____

_____

_____

▶ **Isaiah 53:** From this passage, do you see how everything Isaiah foretold came to pass? Why or why not?

my prayer:

_____

_____

_____

_____

_____

_____

answered prayer:

_____

_____

_____

_____

someone to pray for:

_____

_____

_____

_____

day **24**
God is

communicate

"Who can prove God exists? I have a skeptical friend who refers to the Bible as 'a bunch of fairy tales.' She refuses to believe in God without scientific proof. What can I say?"

You alone are the Lord. You made the heavens, even the highest heavens, and all their starry host, the earth and all that is on it, the seas and all that is in them. You give life to everything, and the multitudes of heaven worship you.

NEHEMIAH 9:6

experience **Him**

Brace yourself—because you probably won't like our answer. The truth is, God's existence can't be proved. (At least, scientifically.) Believing in God and knowing Him personally is a heart thing, not a head thing. If your friend's heart is hardened toward Him, then none of it will make sense to her.

Consider telling her this: We can't prove the existence of some of God's more famous human creations—people like C. S. Lewis, George Washington, or King Tutankhamen (aka King Tut). Photographs, dollar bills, and ancient artwork provide evidence that these humans existed—but not proof. Evidence points to fact. Proof asserts a fact irrefutably.

On the other hand, we can put a droplet of blood under a microscope and, through observation, give irrefutable proof (what scientists call empirical proof) of the identity of this fluid. We can even match it to a specific human or animal.

But we can't give empirical proof that God, C. S. Lewis, George Washington, or King Tut ever existed.

However, the weight of historical evidence not only makes it possible to believe in God's existence—it makes it very hard to ignore.

share Him

God is who He is. We doubt that all the arm twisting or eloquent speeches can convince a non-believing friend that all of creation belongs to God. (In fact, arm-twisting and eloquent speeches aren't exactly God's style.) Transforming a hardened heart is actually the work of God Himself. Besides, proving His existence isn't as important as telling the world what you know of His awesome nature:

▶ God is the sovereign Lord of Scripture who speaks to men through His Word, acts in His creation and in history, and involves Himself in the lives of His people.

- God is the Shepherd who guides (Genesis 48:15), the Lord who provides (Genesis 22:8), the Voice who brings peace during life's storms (Judges 6:23), the Physician who heals the sick (Exodus 15:26), and the Banner that guides the soldier (Exodus 17:8–16).

- God is the Alpha and the Omega, "the Beginning and the End" (Revelation 21:6).

- God is Immanuel, "God with us" (Matthew 1:23).

- God is our Father (Isaiah 9:6).

- God is holy (1 Samuel 2:2).

- God is love (1 John 4:16).

- God Is (Exodus 3:14).

interactive journal

- **Exodus 3:1–15:** What does this passage tell you about God's character?

_____

_____

_____

_____

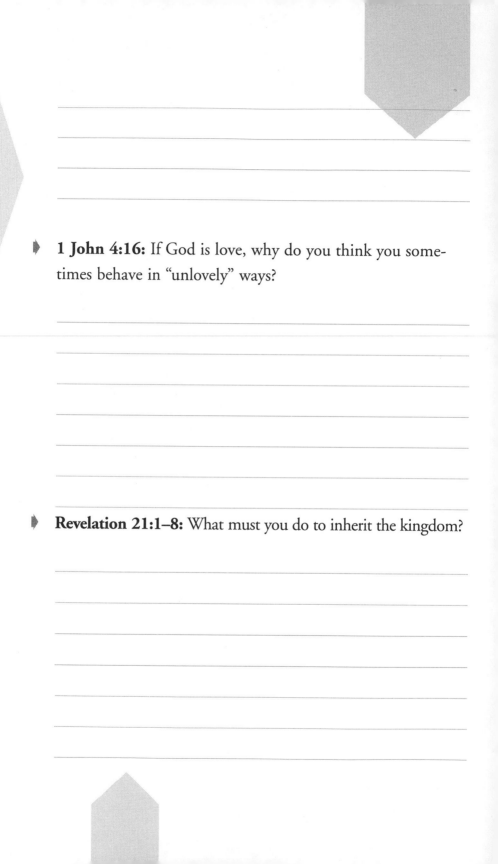

▶ **1 John 4:16:** If God is love, why do you think you sometimes behave in "unlovely" ways?

▶ **Revelation 21:1–8:** What must you do to inherit the kingdom?

my prayer:

answered prayer:

someone to pray for:

day 25
the Holy Spirit guides

communicate

"I want to be more in tune with the Holy Spirit—especially as I step out as Christ's witness. How can I turn down the volume on all the voices of the world, and turn up the volume to the voice of the Holy Spirit?"

"You will receive power when the Holy Spirit comes on you; and you will be my witnesses."

ACTS 1:8

experience Him

Be assured: Your Savior wants to make His presence known in your life. And His Holy Spirit is eager to teach you.

Jesus is here in spirit. Before Jesus left, He promised: "I will ask the Father, and he will give you another Counselor to be with you forever—the Spirit of truth" (John 14:16–17).

Jesus' Spirit lives in the hearts of believers, counseling, comforting, guiding, and teaching. The Spirit will make it plain what following Jesus looks like—one step at a time. But He doesn't yell. The Spirit speaks in a quiet voice. You've got to stop to listen. Often.

Consider people in the Bible such as Adam and Eve, Abraham, Noah, and Moses. One clear thing comes through. They listened to God. They waited for Him to speak. They learned to recognize so clearly the voice of their loving heavenly Father that when God spoke, they knew exactly what God wanted them to do.

Too often, we crowd out God's voice from our lives. We fill our personal worlds with TV, video games, friends, the radio and CD player, the telephone, the Internet. We spend more time plugging into our information-driven culture than we do connecting with God. Yet He speaks to our lives and our hearts daily. The Holy Spirit whispers to our conscience even if we choose to drown Him out.

share Him

Can you sense the Holy Spirit's presence in your life? Can you hear His voice directing your steps?

▸ Seek to experience all the goals and plans God has for you.

▸ Call out to the Holy Spirit for guidance and follow the instruction God has given us through the Scriptures.

interactive journal

▶ **Joel 2:28–32:** Who receives the Holy Spirit?

_____

_____

_____

_____

_____

_____

_____

_____

▶ **Acts 2:1–22:** How does the Holy Spirit guide each of us?

_____

_____

_____

_____

_____

_____

_____

my prayer:

_____
_____
_____
_____
_____
_____

answered prayer:

_____
_____
_____
_____

someone to pray for:

_____
_____
_____
_____

day **26**

the power of prayer

communicate

"Why pray? I mean, if God knows everything—our past, present, and future—and if He understands our every need and shortcomings, why do we need to pray?"

Devote yourselves to prayer, being watchful and thankful. And pray for us, too, that God may open a door for our message, so that we may proclaim the mystery of Christ, for which I am in chains. Pray that I may proclaim it clearly, as I should. Be wise in the way you act toward outsiders; make the most of every opportunity. Let your conversation be always full of grace, seasoned with salt, so that you may know how to answer everyone.

COLOSSIANS 4:2–6

experience Him

God said, "Be still, and know that I am God" (Psalm 46:10). In other words, we need to shut up, slow down, and listen for the voice of God. And Paul was serious when he wrote; "Pray continually" (1 Thessalonians 5:17). Jesus wants you conversing with Him all day long. Consider these thoughts about prayer:

- You don't need to be in church.

- You don't need to kneel.

- You don't need to do anything with your hands.

- You don't even have to raise your voice.

So, why pray? C. S. Lewis has an answer. In his writing *The Efficacy of Prayer*, he explains: "Can we believe that God really modifies His action in response to the suggestions of men? For infinite wisdom does not need telling what is best, and infinite goodness needs no urging to do it."

In other words, the reason God wants us to pray is as simple as it is profound and awe-inspiring: The Lord wants to involve us in the "process." As Pascal said (quoted by Lewis in the same essay), "God instituted prayer in order to lend to His creatures the dignity of causality." God in His infinite wisdom has chosen to grant us the honor of participating in His works.

share Him

- Don't make excuses—just do it! There's no real formula for how you're supposed to pray. Prayer is simply a conversation between you and God. You share what's on your heart, and God shares what's on His. A real conversation!

- Through prayer, we can worship and praise God, confess our sins and repent of them. We can also submit our requests, learn His will for us and seek His help. Jeremiah 29:11–13: " 'For I know the plans I have for you,' declares the Lord, 'plans to prosper you and not to harm you, plans to give you hope and a future. Then you will call upon me and come and pray to me, and I will listen to you. You will seek me and find me when you seek me with all your heart.' "

- Understand that prayer plays a part in bringing others to faith in Christ. Prayer can heal nations and grant us strength to endure trials. (See Isaiah 40:29–31, Hebrews 4:15–16, and 2 Chronicles 7:14.)

- Answered prayer has the potential to be an incredible witness to unbelievers. Skeptics will always have criticisms and doubts regarding answered prayer, but some will see the power of God at work and, as a result, may be drawn to Christ. (See James 5:16 and Colossians 4:2.)

interactive journal

- **Psalm 141:2:** Explain how our prayers are like incense to God.

_____

_____

_____

_____

_____

_____

_____

▶ **James 5:13–18:** What is the prayer of a righteous person?

_____

_____

_____

_____

_____

_____

_____

_____

_____

_____

my prayer:

_____
_____
_____
_____
_____
_____

answered prayer:

_____
_____
_____
_____
_____

someone to pray for:

_____
_____
_____
_____

day **27**
salt and light

communicate

"What is the essence of a true witness? How does God truly want us to go out into the world every day to proclaim the Good News?"

"You are the salt of the earth. But if the salt loses its saltiness, how can it be made salty again? It is no longer good for anything, except to be thrown out and trampled by men. You are the light of the world. A city on a hill cannot be hidden. Neither do people light a lamp and put it under a bowl. Instead they put it on its stand, and it gives light to everyone in the house. In the same way, let your light shine before men, that they may see your good deeds and praise your Father in heaven."

MATTHEW 5:13–16

experience Him

"We are the salt of the earth." What an amazing word picture. What an amazing way to describe the essence of a Christian. And Jesus wants His disciples to understand that following Him means standing up, stepping out, and making a positive, life-changing impact on this mixed-up planet. We simply can't just sit still and keep quiet.

"But if the salt loses its saltiness, how can it be made salty again?" Jesus warns. "It is no longer good for anything, except to be thrown out and trampled by men."

It's safe to say that if most of us knew there wouldn't be any social (or sometimes economic) consequences when we attempt to represent the Christian faith, we wouldn't hesitate to stand up for God. But because there are consequences, many of us keep silent or act wishy-washy.

Instead, be one who counts the cost and boldly goes for it!

share Him

Look at others through Christ's eyes.

▶ Commit to praying for your friends, teachers, and coworkers on a daily basis. (Use the journal part of this book.)

▶ Ask Jesus to show you how to be His hands and feet to hurting teens at your school.

▶ Examine your attitude. Do others notice the truth in you?

Do they know you follow Christ? Do they know you're full of the life, joy, and peace that only God can give?

interactive journal

▸ **2 Corinthians 2:12–3:6:** What does your "letter" tell others about your life?

_____

_____

_____

_____

_____

_____

▸ **2 Timothy 4:1–8:** How can you stay plugged in to the truth?

_____

_____

_____

_____

_____

my prayer:

_____
_____
_____
_____
_____
_____

answered prayer:

_____
_____
_____
_____
_____

someone to pray for:

_____
_____
_____
_____

day **28**
laying down your life

communicate

"I have a friend whose life is going down the drain. What should I do? How can I help?"

"My command is this: Love each other as I have loved you. Greater love has no one than this, that he lay down his life for his friends."

JOHN 15:12–13

experience Him

The night Jesus was betrayed by Judas and deserted by His closest friends, He told them something they'd never forget: The greatest love is shown when a person lays down his life for his friends (John 15:13). Even though Jesus' friends abandoned Him, Jesus still laid down His life for them. That's radical!

When you put your apprehensions aside and actually go do what God wants you to do, you're laying down your life for your friends. When you value your friends over your feelings of embarrassment and stupidity, you are living out the sacrificial love of Jesus. And that's nothing to feel embarrassed or stupid about. . .just ask Jesus.

Jesus was betrayed for a few shiny coins by someone who was supposed to be His friend. There are a lot of Judases today, and chances are you have a few of them as friends. They may not forsake you for thirty pieces of silver. But stuff like drugs, alcohol, sex, stealing, cheating, and lying can prove even more costly to a relationship.

Proverbs 27:6 (NLT) says, "Wounds from a friend are better than many kisses from an enemy." Are you a true friend or a Judas? Are you going to wound your friend or wimp out?

share Him

- Don't preach. Be a friend, but not a parent or pastor.

- Bring a friend. Maybe one or two other friends can help you out. Just make sure everyone knows each other well.

- Start with affirmation. Before you bite into the thick meat of the situation, serve up something easier to swallow, like how important your friend is to you.

- Make it clear you're not condemning, just concerned.

- Be specific. Don't refer to vague situations. Present clear facts based in truth, not rumor or exaggeration.

- Avoid words like always, never, and every. . . . They sound extreme.

- Find a good place to meet that'll be free of distractions.

- Be willing to own up to situations, conflicts, and inconsistencies in your own life that your friend may mention. Honesty is a good bridge-builder.

- Focus on your feelings rather than your friend's failures. He's already going to feel awkward enough without someone beating it into him.

- Be ready to go the distance with your friend. Not everything will change in one meeting. So be willing to meet again and again. Pray for your friend and ask God to give you the wisdom you need!

interactive journal

- **Psalm 133:** How should friends live?

_____

_____

_____

_____

_____

Proverbs 27:1–10: What's the mark of a true friend?

my prayer:

answered prayer:

someone to pray for:

notes

1 Adapted from *Geek-Proof Your Faith* by Greg Johnson and Michael Ross, (Zondervan, 1995), 86–87.

2 Adapted from "Counterculture Christians" by Michael Ross, *Breakaway,* November 1997, and is reprinted with permission of Focus on the Family.

3 Bob Briner, *Roaring Lambs,* (Grand Rapids, Mich.: Zondervan Publishing House, 1993), 29–30.

4 David Watson, *Called and Committed,* (Wheaton, Ill.: Harold Shaw Publishers, 1982), 141.

5 Billy Graham, *Unto the Hills,* (Dallas, Texas: Word Publishing, 1986), 123–24.

6 Adapted from *Faith Encounter* by Bill Myers and Michael Ross, (Harvest House, 1999) 223–24.

7 Adapted from *Speaking of Jesus* 1995 by J. Mack Stiles and InterVarsity Christian Fellowship, 1995.

8 J. I. Packer, *Knowing God* (Downers Grove, Ill.: Inter-Varsity Press, 1973) 15-16.

9 Fritz Ridenour, *So What's the Difference?* (Ventura, Calif.: Regal Books, 2001), 79–80.

10 Charles Stanley, *A Gift of Love,* (Nashville, Tenn.: Thomas Nelson, Nashville, 2001), 191.

11 Henry Blackaby, *Experiencing God,* (Nashville, Tenn.: Broadman & Holman, 1998), 310.

12 C. S. Lewis, *Mere Christianity,* 64.

names and addresses

names and addresses

names and addresses

names and addresses

names and addresses

prayer list

prayer list

prayer list

prayer list

prayer list

_____   _____
_____   _____
_____   _____
_____   _____
_____   _____
_____   _____
_____   _____
_____   _____
_____   _____
_____   _____
_____   _____
_____   _____
_____   _____
_____   _____
_____   _____

prayer list

_____   _____
_____   _____
_____   _____
_____   _____
_____   _____
_____   _____
_____   _____
_____   _____
_____   _____
_____   _____
_____   _____
_____   _____
_____   _____
_____   _____
_____   _____
_____   _____
_____   _____
_____   _____
_____   _____
_____   _____

prayer list

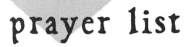
prayer list

_____   _____
_____   _____
_____   _____
_____   _____
_____   _____
_____   _____
_____   _____
_____   _____
_____   _____
_____   _____
_____   _____
_____   _____
_____   _____
_____   _____
_____   _____
_____   _____
_____   _____
_____   _____
_____   _____
_____   _____
_____   _____
_____   _____

the authors

Terry K. Brown is a former nurse and the creator of children's and youth product, including the popular *TodaysGirls.com* and the Today's Girl (Tommy Nelson) book series. She lives in Muncie, Indiana, with her husband and three teenage sons.

Michael Ross is the editor of Focus on the Family's *Breakaway* magazine. He is also the author of several books for young people and families, including *Geek-Proof Your Faith* (Zondervan) and *Faith Encounter* (Harvest House). Michael lives in Colorado Springs, Colorado, with his wife.